Best Hikes and
Nature Walks
With Kids
In and Around
Southwestern
British Columbia

An arbutus tree at
Dorman Point (Hike 38).

Stephen Hui

Foreword by **MYIA ANTONE**

Best Hikes

AND

NATURE WALKS

WITH KIDS

IN AND AROUND SOUTHWESTERN BRITISH COLUMBIA

GREYSTONE BOOKS

Vancouver/Berkeley/London

*For my son, Ollie, who helps me slow down
and see the trees for the forest,
and for all the teachers going the extra mile
for outdoor education*

Greystone Books Ltd.
greystonebooks.com

Cataloguing data available from Library and Archives Canada
ISBN 978-1-77164-597-3 (pbk.)
ISBN 978-1-77164-598-0 (epub)

Editing by Lucy Kenward
Copy editing by Erin Parker
Proofreading by Alison Strobel
Indexing by Stephen Ullstrom

Cover and text design by Jessica Sullivan
Cover photographs by Stephen Hui (top front; back), Michael Leyne
(bottom front), Tomasz Czadowski/Shutterstock.com (inset front)
Photographs by Stephen Hui, except where credited otherwise
Maps created by Richard Vladars

Printed and bound in Singapore on FSC® certified paper at COS Printers Pte Ltd. The
FSC® label means that materials used for the product have been responsibly sourced.

Greystone Books gratefully acknowledges the Musqueam, Squamish, and
Tsleil-Waututh peoples on whose land our Vancouver head office is located.

Greystone Books thanks the Canada Council for the Arts, the British Columbia
Arts Council, the Province of British Columbia through the Book Publishing Tax
Credit, and the Government of Canada for supporting our publishing activities.

WATERFALLS ARE DANGEROUS!

Each year, people fall or are swept to their deaths at waterfalls. Fast water, slippery rocks, unstable surfaces and the vertical heights are all hazards to be avoided.

For your safety, enjoy the falls from a safe viewing distance.

Do not climb above or swim around the falls.

BC Parks

A warning in Golden Ears Provincial Park.

Safety Notice

Hiking and all forms of outdoor recreation involve inherent risks and an element of unpredictability. Many of the hikes in this guidebook are not for novices and may not be safe for your party. There are dangers on every trail, route, and road, and conditions can change at any time. While every effort has been made to ensure accuracy, this book may contain errors. You assume full responsibility for your safety and health in the backcountry. The author, publisher, and distributors accept no liability for any loss, damage, injury, or death arising from the use of this book. Check current conditions, carry the 10 essentials, exercise caution, and stay within your limits.

Frosty Mountain and Lightning Lake from Rainbow Bridge (Hike 37).

Contents

Old-growth trees on the Giant Fir Trail (Hike 5).

Ancient sentinels

These Douglas firs have survived centuries of challenges, from fierce storms to raging fires, and attacks by insects, fungus and disease.

They also escaped the axes and saws of logging in the early 1900s.

Today, they're protected as part of Capilano River Regional Park -- but they still face challenges.

Footsteps compact the soil and can damage the tree's roots and its ability to get water and nutrients.

So, while you might be tempted to get closer to the trees, we ask that you stay behind the fence.

Thanks for helping us protect these ancient trees!

Foreword • MYIA ANTONE

TA NÉWYAP! Hi, everyone! What an honour to share this space with you. When I close my eyes, I picture families and friends smiling and laughing while being outside. Embracing a notion of community that doesn't just include each other, but the surrounding nature that makes us whole. A community that takes care of one another and takes care of their home. Because in community, we are all responsible for each other. When I open my eyes, I can feel that sense of love and joy—and I am continuously working to make sure everyone understands that community includes the animals, plants, and water that we share these lands with.

We all get outside for different reasons. As a Sḵwx̱wú7mesh slhánay̓ (Squamish woman), I get outside to connect with the lands and waters that my ancestors have protected since time began. We take care of these lands because our culture, language, and identity are so intertwined with the landscape around us. We would not be who we are without the rivers, trees, ocean, or mountains. We also all have a role to play in the kinship of our communities. Our smenmánit (mountains), stséḵtseḵ (forests), staḵw (rivers), s7uḵw'uḵw'íńexw (animals), and méńmen (children) carry different gifts, and each have something important to offer this world. We have so much to learn from our méńmen, and we are often reminded of their gifts when we spend time outside with them.

I participated in a land-based education program that understood the importance of getting children outside. While their parents sat around the fire, learning Indigenous languages and listening to Indigenous scholars, the children learned from their aunties and uncles how to walk gently on this Earth. They then would teach us their new skills and knowledge, and remind us of the reciprocal relationship we must have with the land and each other. For knowledge is meant to be shared.

I wholeheartedly believe that kids belong in nature: the land being their classroom and also their greatest teacher. It is important to disconnect to be able to connect. When you are outside, you have the opportunity to listen closely. Quiet your mind and listen to the world interact around you. Listen to the stories of the ancestors who have been here since time out of mind. Stories that remind you how to be a good person and how to be in relationship with everything around you. We are all storytellers, and we each have our own stories to tell.

Please walk gently on these lands and waters, as our children do. Respect those who came before you, and prepare for those who will come after. And remember, the best thank-you to someone who has taught you something is to teach and share that knowledge with someone else. Reciprocity is the foundation of our way of being.

MYIA ANTONE *is a youth from Sḵwx̱wú7mesh Úxwumixw (Squamish Nation) and is based in her hometown of Squamish, B.C. She is a Sḵwx̱wú7mesh sníchim (Squamish language) lifelong learner and teacher, and is passionate about land-based education and language revitalization. Antone is the founder of Indigenous Women Outdoors, a community-led organization that supports Indigenous women and non-binary community members get back out on the land.*

Preface

‖‖

FILLING MY LUNGS with cool mountain air, I lead my five-year-old son, Ollie, into the North Shore woods. My racing mind begins to settle down as we bask in the sound of Lynn Creek and stare up at towering trees.

"Let's go home, Dad," my son pipes up, interrupting my reverie—after what feels like 15 minutes on the trail.

"Home is that way," I answer, pointing deeper into the forest. I'm not fibbing, I tell myself. After all, we are doing a loop.

My son eyes me with suspicion. But he follows as I continue up the trail.

After an hour of hiking, he's having a blast—running across little bridges, boulder hopping, imitating Douglas squirrel cheeps, finding walking sticks, and asking if every large Douglas-fir is a "grandpa tree."

By trail's end, he's pooped and requesting ice cream. On the way back to the bus stop, we order strawberry scoops at the general store outside the park entrance.

I WROTE and researched this guidebook while my son was between the ages of six and eight.

Starting with his first hike, the parks along Lynn Creek in North Vancouver—Lynn Headwaters Regional Park, the Lower Seymour Conservation Reserve, and Lynn Canyon Park—became our go-to destination due to their interconnected network of family-friendly trails and convenient transit access. (Lynn Creek is known as X̱a7élcha Swa7lt in Sḵwx̱wú7mesh sníchim to the Squamish Nation and Kan-ul-cha in hən̓q̓əmin̓əm̓ to the Tsleil-Waututh Nation.)

Hiking with my son has led me to stop and smell the wildflowers more, so to speak, and see and hear the forest with fresh eyes and ears. It's also redoubled my appreciation for the teachers, Scout leaders, and camp counsellors who put in the time and effort to provide the outdoor education and recreation opportunities that evidently left a lasting impression on me during my youth.

This guide is intended to help adults—including parents, guardians, relatives, friends, and educators—introduce kids to the joys of hiking. Hikers of all ages and experience levels, however, should find trails of interest among the short and easy trips highlighted in these pages.

So, pick a hike, be safe, tread lightly, and have fun. I hope you enjoy these trails as much as I do.

Introduction

||||||||||||||||||||||||||||||||||||||||||||||||||||||||||||||||||||||||||||||||||||||||||||

DO YOU REMEMBER the first time you saw a waterfall? Smelled skunk cabbage? Heard a bald eagle's call? Stood beneath an old-growth tree? When you take a hike with young kids, you get to experience the magic of discovering nature all over again. It's a golden opportunity to create beautiful memories, expand their understanding of the world, and build self-confidence. Plus, it's the perfect antidote to all that screen time.

However, hiking with kids is a very different animal than getting outside with adults. For one thing, kids tend to be slower, more easily distracted, and, when little, less steady. Choosing a hike calls for an adjustment in criteria—not just less distance and elevation gain (see Hiking With Kids, p. 19).

Best Hikes and Nature Walks With Kids In and Around Southwestern British Columbia is your guide to navigating this world. I selected the 55 hikes in this book with children aged 4 to 11 in mind. All of these trips feature points of particular interest to kids—hollow trees, suspension bridges, tide pools, etc. The kid-focused difficulty ratings are intended to help you thoughtfully introduce children to the challenges of backcountry travel, starting with trails where kids can mostly walk and explore on their own and adults don't need to be hypervigilant about trail hazards (see How to Use This Guide, p. 25).

This cross-border guide features family-friendly hikes north, east, west, and south of Vancouver, B.C.—from Victoria to E.C. Manning

The viewpoint at North Point (Hike 44).

Provincial Park and Duffey Lake to Deception Pass in northwestern Washington. It highlights well-trafficked crowd-pleasers—Skookumchuck Narrows (Hike 44) and Train Wreck Falls (Hike 16), for example—and quieter local favourites, such as the Echo Valley Trail (Hike 47) and Hoover Lake (Hike 29).

All of the outings featured in this book are distinct from those of *105 Hikes In and Around Southwestern British Columbia* and *Destination Hikes In and Around Southwestern British Columbia*, which cover many of the same regions. The selected hikes fit within the following parameters (with a few exceptions):

- Are accessible as a day or weekend trip from Vancouver.
- Are doable with kids in a short day on foot.
- Cover a total distance between 2 km (1.2 mi) and 12 km (7.5 mi).
- Offer some elevation change (up to a net elevation gain of 350 m [1,150 ft]); for instance, dike trails are not included.
- Emphasize natural environments over urban settings, and rustic trails and logging roads over paved surfaces.
- Require no more than simple Class 2 terrain. (In the Yosemite Decimal System, Class 1 denotes foot travel; Class 2 involves some use of hands; Class 3 entails scrambling with mild exposure.)

Infants and toddlers can enjoy these trails from the comfort of a baby carrier or specialized backpack, worn by an adult. Due to narrow paths, uneven surfaces, steep grades, and obstacles, these hikes are generally not recommended for strollers (including all-terrain models) and wheelchairs. Bikes and scooters are better left at home too—adults often end up carrying a tired kid's wheels.

Vancouver, at the heart of this guide, lies in the Indigenous territories of the Musqueam (xʷməθkʷəy̓əm), Squamish (S̱ḵwx̱wú7mesh), and Tsleil-Waututh (səlilwətaɬ) First Nations. The trails in this book traverse the territories of the Coast Salish, Nlaka'pamux, St'át'imc, and Syilx peoples, who have stewarded these lands and waters since time immemorial. These territories are home to an incredible diversity of Indigenous languages and dialects: Halq'eméylem, hən̓q̓əmin̓əm̓, and Hul'q'umi'num'; Lushootseed; Nɬeʔkepmxcín; Nsyilxcən; SENĆOŦEN, Xwlemi'chosen, and Xws7ámeshqen; sháshíshálem; S̱ḵwx̱wú7mesh sníchim; and Ucwalmícwts. Many mountains, islands, lakes, and rivers bear Indigenous names, new and old. Important cultural sites dot the landscape.

Respect these special places as you explore this corner of Planet Earth. Let the old maxim "Take only photographs, leave only footprints" guide you (see Safety, Ethics, and Etiquette, p. 21). Please add your voice to calls for increases to funding and rangers for parks and trails, and new and expanded protected areas. Let's preserve public lands for wildlife, non-motorized recreation, First Nations cultural values, and future generations.

I welcome your feedback, as well as trail and access updates, via 105hikes.com. Happy trails!

Graffiti covers a derelict cabin at Parkhurst (Hike 18).

Hiking With Kids

||||||||||||||||||||||||||||||||||||||||||||||||||||||||||||||||||||||||||||||||||

HITTING THE TRAIL with kids can be both gratifying and exasperating, and comes with its own special charms and challenges. Get off on the right foot and you might have a hiking buddy for life. Don't get off on the wrong foot. Here are several tips for hiking with kids.

Pick the right trail A pre-tween might struggle on a path that a preschooler rockets up. Regardless of age, start with beginner (●) hikes on wide trails with minimal elevation gain before trying intermediate (■) and challenging (◆) trips. (For additional kid-friendly options, as well as plenty of harder trails, see 105 *Hikes* and *Destination Hikes*.) Choose a trail that appeals to their interests—beavers, big trees, birds, horses, suspension bridges, or trains, for example (see the Best Hikes by Category appendix, p. 228).

Be flexible on the destination Lower your expectations. You may or may not reach the waterfall at trail's end. Hiking with young kids really is about the journey, not the destination.

Reduce your speed Curious kids will stop to investigate every ditch, snail, or spiderweb. Have a closer look yourself and delight in their discoveries.

Take lots of breaks Shorter legs require more steps to cover the same distance. If you never had any use for park benches and picnic tables, you'll appreciate their value now.

Bring food the kids will eat (and plenty of it) Prevent the hangry child. Frequent snacking (and drinking) will help keep kids' energy levels and spirits up. Now's the time to pull out the gummy bears and chocolate chunk cookies. Pack a picnic for lunch. Be sure to carry extra water.

Pack a full change of clothes Kids have a propensity to get wet, and a cold kid is an unhappy kid. Bring warm layers and rain gear too. A toque, mittens, and windbreaker are lifesavers on a windy summit, as is a bug jacket when the insects are biting. Avoid cotton—just like adults, kids need proper footwear and quick-dry clothing. Don't forget the wet wipes and, if applicable, extra diapers.

Be prepared to carry everything While bringing more than sufficient supplies is a good idea—not to mention binoculars, hiking poles, and other optional items—you don't want to overdo it. After all, a tired kid probably won't want anything heavier than fishy crackers and a stuffed orca in their backpack. Keep in mind that circumstances may call on you to carry an exhausted or injured kid out of the woods.

Seek out water Whether it's icicles, lakes, puddles, streams, waterfalls, or waves on a beach, water is a huge hit with kids. Any trail with plenty of opportunities to see, hear, and splash in water is solid gold. Keep kids close and be careful around slippery rocks, swift currents, and deep water.

Give kids a mission Look for the perfect walking stick or magic wand. Search for hollow trees. Try to spot something in each of the primary and secondary colours. Go geocaching. Bring a favourite stuffy for photo ops along the trail. Prepare a list (or use the featured animals, plants, and fungi in the Wild Sights section at the back of the book, p. 212) and make it a scavenger hunt. See, I told you hiking is fun!

Safety, Ethics, and Etiquette

||||||||||||||||||||||||||||||||||||||||||||||||||||||||||||||||||||||||||||||||||||||||||

HELP NURTURE future generations of responsible hikers. Teach kids these important guidelines for sharing the trails.

Carry the 10 essentials

1. *Navigation* (map, compass, GPS)
2. *Headlamp* (extra batteries)
3. *Sun protection* (sunglasses, sunscreen, sun hat, sun-protective clothing)
4. *First aid* (bandages, blister pads, insect-bite remedy, tweezers for ticks)
5. *Knife* (repair kit, duct tape)
6. *Fire* (waterproof matches, lighter)
7. *Shelter* (tent, emergency blanket)
8. *Extra food* (energy bars, trail mix)
9. *Extra water* (purifier)
10. *Extra clothes* (rain gear, insulating layers)

Leave a trip plan Before you go hiking, inform a reliable person of your destination, route, equipment, and expected return time—to help search-and-rescue volunteers find you in the event of an emergency.

Note sunset time It's easy to get lost or injured in the dark, even with a headlamp. Set a safe turnaround time and stick to it.

Keep your distance from drop-offs and wildlife Hold on to young kids in steep terrain and around cliffs. Don't throw stones from heights, roll rocks downhill, or chase wildlife. Stay together to reduce the likelihood of a bear attack or getting lost. (Groups of three or more are less likely to be attacked by a bear. Carry bear spray and use it to repel aggressive wildlife.)

Save the cellphone for emergencies Many of these hikes go out of cellphone range. Unless you carry a personal locator beacon or satellite messenger, however, you'll probably need to seek reception and call for help in an emergency. Keeping your cellphone warm, dry, and powered off helps ensure you have enough battery life to make the all-important call.

Learn the seven principles of Leave No Trace
1. *Plan ahead and prepare*
2. *Travel and camp on durable surfaces*
3. *Dispose of waste properly*
4. *Leave what you find*
5. *Minimize campfire impacts*
6. *Respect wildlife*
7. *Be considerate of other visitors*

Respect the posted regulations These rules are in place to safeguard the natural and cultural values of protected areas. Stay on trails and don't shortcut. Adhere to fire bans. Don't feed wildlife. Drones, flower and mushroom picking, smoking, and vaping are prohibited in the backcountry of provincial parks.

Use toilets where available Where facilities don't exist, bury poop and toilet tissue in a cat hole 15–20 cm (6–8 in) deep and 70 adult paces away from water, trails, and campsites. Always pack out diapers, sanitary pads and tampons, and wet wipes, including allegedly biodegradable products, and dispose of them in the garbage.

Keep dogs on leash (or at home) Even on leash, dogs disrupt the natural patterns of wildlife. Off-leash dogs can harass, injure, and kill wild animals. B.C. Parks discourages taking dogs into the backcountry due to the potential for conflicts with wildlife, including bears. Dogs must be leashed in many provincial parks.

Avoid hiking in large groups In the U.S., regulations limit the size of parties to 12 in wilderness areas. Consider this a general rule for the backcountry. Large groups are more likely to disturb wildlife and other users and cause environmental damage.

Be inclusive Everyone should feel welcome in the outdoors, regardless of age, class, ethnicity, gender, sexual orientation, or size. Nature has no official language.

Yield to other trail users Don't block the path. Let faster parties pass. On narrow trails, downhill hikers should step aside for those travelling uphill. On multi-use trails, mountain bikers yield to hikers and both give way to horse riders. However, it's often easier—and courteous—for hikers to step aside for bikers too.

················· **Get Informed** ·····················

AdventureSmart
adventuresmart.ca

Avalanche Canada
avalanche.ca

B.C. Parks
bcparks.ca

B.C. Search and Rescue Association
bcsara.com

Federation of Mountain Clubs of B.C.
mountainclubs.org

Get Bear Smart Society
bearsmart.com

Leave No Trace Center for Outdoor Ethics
lnt.org

Washington Trails Association
wta.org

The Sooke River at Sand Pebble Beach (Hike 49).

How to Use This Guide

THE 55 HIKES in this book are categorized by regions north, east, west, and south of Vancouver and arranged by distance from the city. To select a hike, start with the Hikes at a Glance table (p. 32) or consult the Best Hikes by Category (p. 228), Hikes by Distance (p. 230), and Hikes by Elevation Gain (p. 232) appendices.

Each numbered trip comes with feature icons, statistics and ratings, a brief summary, driving and hiking directions, a topographic map, and photographs. I've included public transit options where available.

What follows are explanations of the feature icons, statistics, and ratings used in this guide, as well as information to help clarify the driving and hiking directions.

Features

Icons draw your attention to the features of each numbered trip, with a particular emphasis on access and use.

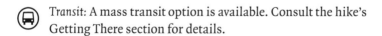 *Transit:* A mass transit option is available. Consult the hike's Getting There section for details.

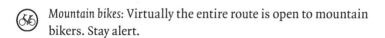 *Mountain bikes:* Virtually the entire route is open to mountain bikers. Stay alert.

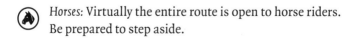 *Horses:* Virtually the entire route is open to horse riders. Be prepared to step aside.

DOGS:

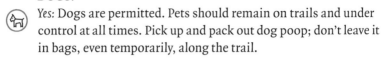 *Yes:* Dogs are permitted. Pets should remain on trails and under control at all times. Pick up and pack out dog poop; don't leave it in bags, even temporarily, along the trail.

Leash required: Dogs must be leashed for all or a portion of the hike. Respect the posted regulations. Hikers with dogs yield to other hikers. Check the hiking directions for details.

No: Dogs are prohibited on all or part of the route. Leave furry friends at home.

Interpretive: Informative panels (at least two, not including signs at the trailhead) shed light on the cultural, ecological, geographical, geological, or historical context of the hike.

Statistics

Time estimates are not provided, as the pace of children varies widely—to put it mildly. Then there are all the investigative stops, snack breaks, photo ops, and other diversions. The point is not to rush.

Distance: The round-trip length of the hike as described is provided in metric and imperial units.

Elevation gain: The net elevation gain is simply the difference between the highest and lowest points encountered on the hike. Although both metric and imperial elevations are noted in the text, the maps show contour lines in metric only.

High point: This statistic represents the highest elevation above mean sea level attained on the hike.

Season: The time of year when conditions are typically—but not always—favourable for the hike is indicated. That is, the trail should be completely or mostly snow-free, so no need for snowshoes or traction aids.

Map: The small maps in this guide are no substitute for large, printed maps. For each hike, a map sheet from Natural Resources Canada's National Topographic System (NTS), the U.S. Geological Survey (USGS), or another publisher is recommended.

Erin's Enchanted Forest (Hike 9)
on Unnecessary Mountain.

Trailhead: The geographic position of the start of the hike is given in degrees, minutes, and seconds using the World Geodetic System 1984 (WGS84) datum. The trailhead is often, but not necessarily, adjacent to the parking area.

Ratings

This book employs a kid-focused rating system that differs from those used by 105 *Hikes* and *Destination Hikes*. Each hike is assigned a difficulty rating and a quality rating. Since hikes with kids must often be flexible on the ultimate destination, distance is not factored into the difficulty ratings. Both ratings are inherently subjective but might help you select the right trip for a given child and day.

Difficulty

● *Beginner:* Mostly wide paths, mild inclines, and few obstacles. Start here.

■ *Intermediate:* Narrow paths, steep sections, and/or some obstacles.

◆ *Challenging:* Rough paths, sustained steep sections, and/or potentially hazardous terrain. Only recommended for kids with hiking experience, good judgment, and self-control.

Quality

☺ *Good:* A nice dose of the outdoors.

☺☺ *Very good:* A rich serving of the wonders of nature. Fun!

☺☺☺ *Outstanding:* An exceptionally delightful experience for kids and adults alike. Super fun!

Getting There

Driving directions are provided from major highways. When vehicle access involves gravel roads, I've noted whether two-wheel drive (2WD), four-wheel drive (4WD), and/or high clearance is required (at time of writing).

The following locations are shorthand for particular intersections:

- *Downtown Squamish:* Highway 99 (Sea to Sky Highway) and Cleveland Avenue/Loggers Lane.
- *Mount Currie:* Main Street and Lillooet Lake Road, where northbound Highway 99 traffic turns right (for Duffey Lake Road).
- *Sechelt Village:* Sunshine Coast Highway/Dolphin Street and Wharf Avenue, where northbound Highway 101 traffic turns left (for Earls Cove).
- *Whistler Village:* Highway 99 (Sea to Sky Highway) and Village Gate Boulevard.

The Hike

Trails are not described in winter conditions. River directions (for example, "river left" and "right bank") are given from the perspective of looking downstream. A "lollipop" hike features a loop at its far end; the same route (the "stem") is followed to the loop and back to the trailhead.

Key to Map Symbols

⚑	trailhead	▬▬▬	described trail
℗	parking	▬▬▬	other trail
🚾	toilet	·-·-·-·	track
▲	camping	═══	road
🌊	waterfall	———	stream/creek
👀	viewpoint	+++++	railroad
🚌	bus stop	o—o—o	ski lift
♠	hut/lodge	·—·—·	power line
4WD	4-wheel-drive road	∿∿	topographic contour
⚠	warning	▀▀▀	park
⊖	no entry		
▲	mountain peak		
99	major highway		
)(	bridge		

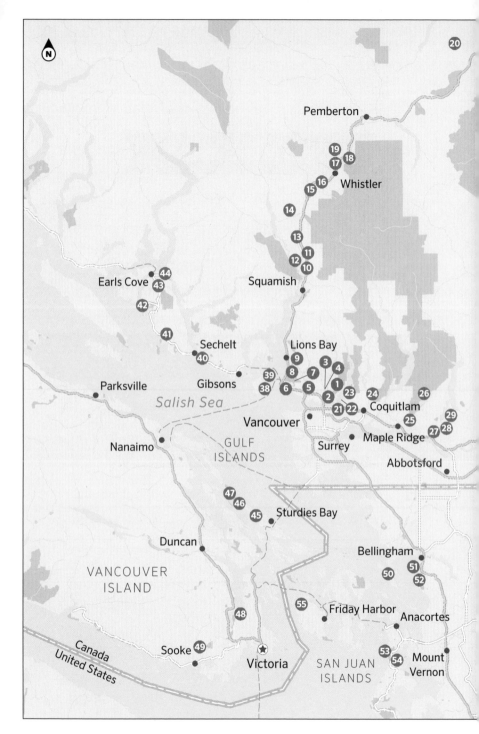

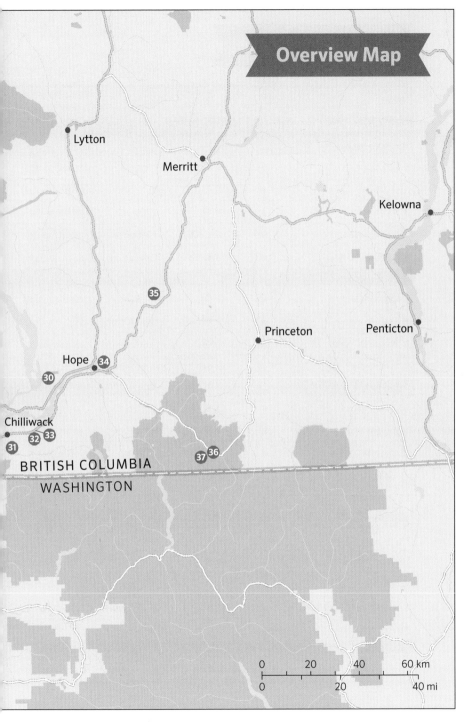

Overview Map

Lytton

Merritt

Kelowna

35

Princeton

Penticton

Hope 34

30

Chilliwack

32 33

31

37 36

BRITISH COLUMBIA

WASHINGTON

0   20   40   60 km

0   20   40 mi

Hikes at a Glance

Hike	Difficulty	Quality	Distance	Elevation Gain
HIKES *NORTH* OF Vancouver				
North Vancouver				
1 Dog Mountain	■	☺ ☺ ☺	4.8 km (3 mi)	45 m (150 ft)
2 Fisherman's Trail	●	☺	16 km (10 mi)	90 m (295 ft)
3 Rice Lake	●	☺ ☺	3 km (1.9 mi)	30 m (100 ft)
4 Lynn Canyon	■	☺ ☺ ☺	3 km (1.9 mi)	170 m (560 ft)
5 Capilano Canyon	●	☺ ☺ ☺	4.1 km (2.5 mi)	60 m (200 ft)
West Vancouver and Lions Bay				
6 Cypress Falls	■	☺ ☺	3 km (1.9 mi)	120 m (390 ft)
7 Lost Lake	◆	☺ ☺	8.5 km (5.3 mi)	180 m (590 ft)
8 Bowen Lookout	●	☺ ☺	4.3 km (2.7 mi)	120 m (390 ft)
9 Erin Moore Trail	◆	☺ ☺	3.2 km (2 mi)	155 m (510 ft)
Squamish				
10 Four Lakes Trail	●	☺ ☺ ☺	6 km (3.7 mi)	120 m (390 ft)
11 Brohm Lake	■	☺ ☺	3.5 km (2.2 mi)	40 m (130 ft)
12 Levette Lake	◆	☺ ☺ ☺	8 km (5 mi)	300 m (985 ft)
13 Cheakamus Canyon	■	☺ ☺	7 km (4.3 mi)	235 m (770 ft)
14 Berg Lake	◆	☺ ☺ ☺	3.9 km (2.4 mi)	140 m (460 ft)
Whistler				
15 Cal-Cheak Trail	■	☺ ☺	3.2 km (2 mi)	45 m (150 ft)
16 Train Wreck Falls	■	☺ ☺ ☺	2.8 km (1.7 mi)	50 m (165 ft)
17 One Duck Lake	◆	☺ ☺	3.2 km (2 mi)	90 m (295 ft)
18 Parkhurst Ghost Town	■	☺ ☺	5.6 km (3.5 mi)	80 m (260 ft)
19 Ancient Cedars Trail	■	☺ ☺	4.7 km (2.9 mi)	189 m (620 ft)
Duffey Lake				
20 Holly Lake	◆	☺ ☺ ☺	4.3 km (2.7 mi)	245 m (800 ft)

Transit	Mountain Bikes	Interpretive	Horses	Dogs
				LEASH
●	●	●		NO
●		●		NO
●		●		LEASH
●		●		LEASH
●				YES
				LEASH
		●		NO
●		●		LEASH
		●		NO
		●		LEASH
				YES
	●			YES
				YES
				LEASH
●	●	●		LEASH
●	●			LEASH
				LEASH
		●		YES
				YES

Hike	Difficulty	Quality	Distance	Elevation Gain
HIKES *EAST* OF Vancouver				
Burnaby to Coquitlam				
21 Burnaby Mountain	◆	☺	6.5 km (4 mi)	290 m (950 ft)
22 Jug Island Beach	■	☺ ☺	5.2 km (3.2 mi)	85 m (280 ft)
23 Sasamat Lake	●	☺ ☺	3.2 km (2 mi)	20 m (65 ft)
24 Woodland Walk	■	☺ ☺	9 km (5.6 mi)	175 m (575 ft)
Maple Ridge				
25 Alouette Valley Trail	●	☺	12 km (7.5 mi)	110 m (360 ft)
26 Lower Falls Trail	●	☺ ☺ ☺	5.7 km (3.5 mi)	115 m (380 ft)
Mission to Harrison Hot Springs				
27 Railway Trail	●	☺	12 km (7.5 mi)	65 m (210 ft)
28 Steelhead Falls	●	☺ ☺	5 km (3.1 mi)	80 m (260 ft)
29 Hoover Lake	■	☺	8 km (5 mi)	300 m (985 ft)
30 Hicks Lake	●	☺	6 km (3.7 mi)	45 m (150 ft)
Chilliwack				
31 Mount Thom	■	☺ ☺	7 km (4.3 mi)	290 m (950 ft)
32 Three Bears	●	☺ ☺ ☺	2.3 km (1.4 mi)	50 m (165 ft)
33 Thaletel Trail	◆	☺	5.4 km (3.4 mi)	250 m (820 ft)
Hope and Coquihalla Pass				
34 Thacker Mountain	■	☺ ☺	4.8 km (3 mi)	130 m (430 ft)
35 Little Douglas Lake	■	☺ ☺	3.2 km (2 mi)	90 m (295 ft)
E.C. Manning Provincial Park				
36 Similkameen Trail	●	☺	4.8 km (3 mi)	30 m (100 ft)
37 Flash Lake	●	☺ ☺	10 km (6.2 mi)	45 m (150 ft)

Transit	Mountain Bikes	Interpretive	Horses	Dogs
•		•		LEASH
•				LEASH
•				LEASH
				LEASH
			•	LEASH
•				LEASH
	•	•		LEASH
				LEASH
				LEASH
				LEASH
•				LEASH
	•	•		YES
	•	•		LEASH
	•			LEASH
				YES
	•		•	LEASH
				LEASH

Hike	Difficulty	Quality	Distance	Elevation Gain
HIKES *WEST* OF Vancouver				
Howe Sound				
38 Dorman Point	▪	☺ ☺	2.4 km (1.5 mi)	100 m (330 ft)
39 Killarney Lake	●	☺ ☺ ☺	8 km (5 mi)	60 m (200 ft)
Sunshine Coast				
40 Chapman Falls	●	☺ ☺ ☺	9 km (5.6 mi)	120 m (390 ft)
41 Homesite Caves	▪	☺ ☺	1.4 km (0.9 mi)	40 m (130 ft)
42 Pender Hill	◆	☺ ☺ ☺	1.6 km (1 mi)	170 m (560 ft)
43 Klein Lake	▪	☺ ☺	6.5 km (4 mi)	150 m (490 ft)
44 Skookumchuck Narrows	●	☺ ☺ ☺	8 km (5 mi)	60 m (200 ft)
Gulf Islands				
45 Gray Peninsula	●	☺ ☺ ☺	2.2 km (1.4 mi)	40 m (130 ft)
46 Pebble Beach	▪	☺ ☺ ☺	6.5 km (4 mi)	75 m (250 ft)
47 Echo Valley Trail	●	☺ ☺	4.2 km (2.6 mi)	65 m (210 ft)
Victoria				
48 McKenzie Bight	▪	☺ ☺ ☺	3 km (1.9 mi)	150 m (490 ft)
49 Sooke Potholes	●	☺ ☺ ☺	4.2 km (2.6 mi)	60 m (200 ft)
HIKES *SOUTH* OF Vancouver				
Bellingham				
50 Lummi Peak	◆	☺ ☺	5.3 km (3.3 mi)	310 m (1,020 ft)
51 Chuckanut Falls	▪	☺	3.8 km (2.4 mi)	100 m (330 ft)
52 Teddy Bear Cove	▪	☺ ☺ ☺	2.6 km (1.6 mi)	65 m (210 ft)
Anacortes and San Juan Islands				
53 Rosario Head	●	☺ ☺ ☺	2.8 km (1.7 mi)	30 m (100 ft)
54 Goose Rock	▪	☺ ☺ ☺	3.6 km (2.2 mi)	148 m (484 ft)
55 Young Hill	▪	☺ ☺	3.2 km (2 mi)	170 m (560 ft)

Transit	Mountain Bikes	Interpretive	Horses	 Dogs
●				LEASH
●				LEASH
	●			YES
				LEASH
				LEASH
	●			LEASH
		●		LEASH
				LEASH
		●		YES
				LEASH
	●		●	LEASH
				LEASH
				NO
	●			LEASH
				LEASH
		●		LEASH
				LEASH
●		●		LEASH

1 Dog Mountain

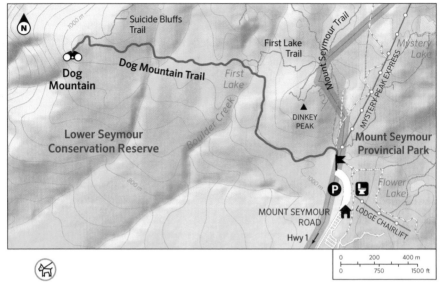

Distance: 4.8 km (3 mi)
Elevation gain: 45 m (150 ft)
High point: 1,054 m (3,460 ft)
Season: late spring to early fall

Difficulty: ■
Quality: ☺☺☺
Map: Trail Ventures BC North Shore
Trailhead: 49°22'03" N, 122°56'57" W

DOG MOUNTAIN is a treat in any season and ideal for an after-work jaunt with the kids. According to the B.C. Archives, the mini summit on a shoulder of Mount Seymour was previously called Dogshead Mountain because it resembles the profile of a St. Bernard—fittingly, a breed known for its alpine rescue work—after a snowfall. Pack a picnic and be prepared to point out notable Vancouver landmarks from high above the cityscape.

GETTING THERE

Vehicle: Westbound on Trans-Canada Highway 1 in North Vancouver, north of Ironworkers Memorial Second Narrows Crossing, take Exit 22B. Turn right on Mount Seymour Parkway. (Eastbound on

Highway 1, take Exit 21. Go left on East Keith Road and right on Mount Seymour Parkway.) In 4.4 km (2.7 mi), turn left on Mount Seymour Road. Drive 12.5 km (7.8 mi) up to the ski area in Mount Seymour Provincial Park. Winter tires or chains are required from October to March. Park as close as you can to the top (toilet available). The gate beyond Parking Lot 2 is closed from dusk till dawn.

THE HIKE

Find the B.C. Parks kiosk at the top of Parking Lot 4. Briefly head north on the Mount Seymour Trail, left of the Mystery Peak Express chairlift and the pond known as Loch Lomond. Turn left at the first opportunity to start the Dog Mountain Trail, adopted by the North Shore Hikers, and enter the Lower Seymour Conservation Reserve, administered by Metro Vancouver.

Immediately, go across a bridge over a creek and by a granitic erratic. Orange squares (and bamboo stakes in winter) denote the undulating, rooty, and rocky path through lovely cedar and fir trees. Step over streamlets; larger creeks are crossed via little bridges and culverts. The trees open up, and you descend to a key junction at First Lake (49°22′20″ N, 122°57′21″ W), after 1 km (0.6 mi) on foot. It's an especially pretty sight when partially frozen.

A right turn on the First Lake Trail offers access to Dinkey Peak en route to the Mount Seymour Trail. However, cross the bridge ahead over the Boulder Creek outlet and keep left on the Dog Mountain Trail on the far side of First Lake. Pass a pond, crossing its outflow on a log.

Keep left at an easy-to-miss junction with the rough and challenging route to Suicide Bluffs. Stick your heads in a holey fir tree and look up its amazing hollow trunk. Arrive at Dog Mountain (49°22′26″ N, 122°58′13″ W), 2.4 km (1.5 mi) from the trailhead. Bask in the remarkable city view from the rocky lookout. Ask the kids what landmarks they recognize from above.

To the southwest, Downtown Vancouver and Stanley Park stand in contrast on the Coal Peninsula, which juts into Burrard Inlet (Slíl̓utulh to the Squamish Nation, Tsleil-Wat to the Tsleil-Waututh Nation). Due west, Mount Fromme reclines across the valley of the Seymour River (Ch'ích'elxwi7k̲w Stak̲w to the Squamish, Jol-gul-hook to the Tsleil-Waututh). Ravens and whisky-jacks will probably drop in for lunch. Don't feed the wildlife.

Downtown Vancouver as seen through the clouds from Dog Mountain.

Dog Mountain lies in the territories of the Musqueam, Squamish, and Tsleil-Waututh First Nations. It's outside the Mount Seymour ski area, so it's free to snowshoe, though backcountry users are limited to less-convenient parking lots 1 and 5 in winter. No camping, drones, fires, horses, mountain biking, smoking, or vaping. Dogs must be leashed. However, B.C. Parks advises that the backcountry is "not suitable" for dogs due to their impact on wildlife and the potential for problems with bears.

···················· **Fun Fact** ····················

A glacial erratic is a rock that a glacier or iceberg has carried a long way—sometimes hundreds of kilometres—from where it started. Ranging from tiny pebbles to house-sized boulders, these out-of-place rocks are left behind when the ice melts. They are often made up of different minerals than the surface on which they are found.

2 Fisherman's Trail

Distance: 16 km (10 mi)	**Difficulty:** ●
Elevation gain: 90 m (295 ft)	**Quality:** ☺
High point: 170 m (560 ft)	**Map:** Trail Ventures BC North Shore
Season: all year	**Trailhead:** 49°19′53″ N, 122°59′59″ W

A ROCKSLIDE partially dammed the Seymour River (Ch'ích'elxwi7ḵw Staḵw to the Squamish Nation, Jol-gul-hook to the Tsleil-Waututh Nation) in 2014, overflowing the concrete crossing at Twin Bridges and severing the Fisherman's Trail. Fortunately, Metro Vancouver built the superb Seymour River Suspension Bridge at this spot four years later, reconnecting the riverside path.

GETTING THERE

Transit: Take TransLink Bus 214 (Blueridge) from Phibbs Exchange to Berkley Avenue at Hyannis Drive (at Blueridge Park). Walk one block northeast on Hyannis.

Vehicle: Westbound on Trans-Canada Highway 1 in North Vancouver, north of Ironworkers Memorial Second Narrows Crossing, take Exit 22B. Turn right on Mount Seymour Parkway. (Eastbound on Highway 1, take Exit 21. Go left on East Keith Road and right on Mount Seymour Parkway.) After 1.7 km (1.1 mi) on the parkway, make a left on Berkley Road. In 2.1 km (1.3 mi), turn left on Hyannis Drive. Find a legal parking spot near the Hyannis Point intersection.

THE HIKE

From the corner of Hyannis Drive and Hyannis Point, head north into the lovely woods on the Hyannis Trail. Stay alert for mountain bikers and don't block the path. Keep left at several junctions to descend the Bridle Trail. Meet the Fisherman's Trail at the Seymour Canyon rockslide site, after 1 km (0.6 mi) of hiking.

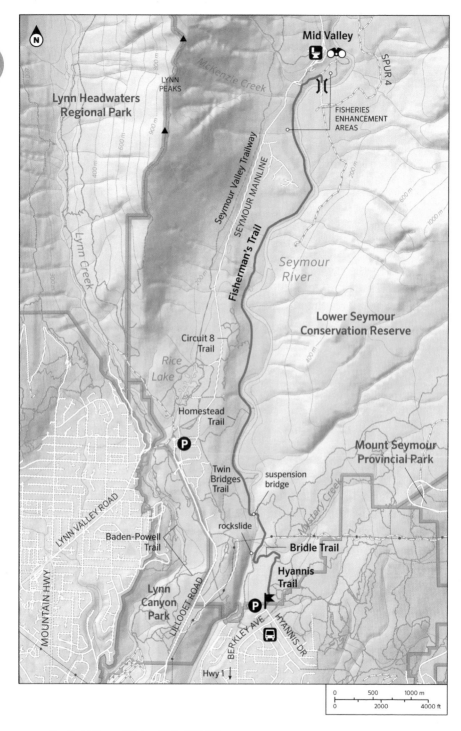

N

Mid Valley

LYNN
PEAKS

**Lynn Headwaters
Regional Park**

McKenzie Creek

SPUR 4

FISHERIES
ENHANCEMENT
AREAS

Seymour Valley Trailway

SEYMOUR MAINLINE

Fisherman's Trail

*Seymour
River*

Lynn Creek

**Lower Seymour
Conservation Reserve**

Circuit 8
Trail

*Rice
Lake*

Homestead
Trail

P

**Mount Seymour
Provincial Park**

Twin
Bridges
Trail

suspension
bridge

Mystery Creek

LYNN VALLEY ROAD

Baden-Powell
Trail

rockslide

Bridle Trail

**Hyannis
Trail**

MOUNTAIN HWY

**Lynn
Canyon
Park**

LILLOOET ROAD

P

BERKLEY AVE

HYANNIS DR

Hwy 1 ↓

0		500		1000 m
0		2000		4000 ft

The Seymour River Suspension Bridge was built in 2018.

Turn right, sticking with Fisherman's, an old logging road, on your way upstream. Take a bridge over Mystery Creek and pass the Mystery Creek Trail. As you approach the Seymour River Suspension Bridge, spot the Bottle Top path leaving to the right. Cross to river right on the bridge, which is higher and longer than its three predecessors and accommodates 100 pedestrians or two horses plus riders. Enjoy the elevated view, which my son describes as "awesome." (For a short outing, turn around here.)

Keep right at the Twin Bridges Trail junction at the west end of the span. Spur 4, our destination, is 6.5 km (4 mi) north. Soon, an aging interpretive panel prompts you to notice a spooky old water pipeline tunnel behind you. (If you bring a flashlight, you can make your way through it.) The escarpment on the left poses a high risk of slides along several sections of the wide gravel trail. Old wooden posts on the right indicate the remains of former homesteads.

Go past the No Dogs Beyond This Point sign at the Homestead Trail junction, continuing upstream on Fisherman's. Ignore the Circuit 8 Trail turnoff. Henceforth, you're more likely to encounter mountain bikers and trail runners than hikers. Go over streams on concrete bridges. Pass a salmon spawning and rearing habitat area at Coho Creek. See if you can spot some fish.

Eventually, Fisherman's rises to meet the Spur 4 road. A connector trail straight ahead leads to the Mid Valley lookout. However, turn right and head down to the Spur 4 Bridge (49°23′26″ N, 122°59′24″ W), noticing double tracks going left by a wetland en route. Stop and listen to the river and take in the upstream and downstream views. Lynn Peaks rise to the west and Mount Seymour to the east.

If you made it this far, it's worth rambling down the aforementioned double tracks to explore the Mid Valley fisheries enhancement area. There are plenty of birds to spot, and salmonberries and thimbleberries too. The peaceful paths combine to make a figure eight—if they're not flooded or too overgrown.

When you're ready to head back, retrace your steps to the suspension bridge and Hyannis Drive. If the kids still have energy to burn, Blueridge Park, near the trailhead, has a playground.

Once considered part of the Seymour Watershed and therefore closed to the public, the Lower Seymour Conservation Reserve opened for recreation in 1987. It lies in the territories of the Musqueam, Squamish, and Tsleil-Waututh First Nations and remains a potential site for a future reservoir. No camping, drones, fires, flower or mushroom picking, smoking, or vaping. Dogs and horses are prohibited north of the Homestead Trail.

···················· **Fun Fact** ·····················
The Seymour Watershed supplies a third of Metro Vancouver's drinking water. The water comes from Seymour Lake, which is held back by the Seymour Falls Dam (built in 1961), upstream of the Lower Seymour Conservation Reserve.

3 ◣ Rice Lake | Trail map on p. 48

Distance: 3 km (1.9 mi)
Elevation gain: 30 m (100 ft)
High point: 220 m (720 ft)
Season: all year

Difficulty: ●
Quality: ☺ ☺
Map: Trail Ventures BC North Shore
Trailhead: 49°21′01″ N, 123°00′52″ W

ONCE UPON A TIME, my son and I got to release a few triploid rainbow trout into Rice Lake as part of a Freshwater Fisheries Society of B.C. event. We watched in awe as a bald eagle swooped down and caught one of the freshly stocked fish. Interpretive panels on the delightfully easy Rice Lake Loop Trail, in the Lower Seymour Conservation Reserve, highlight the lake's history of human interference. In all seasons and weather, Rice Lake is a family favourite.

GETTING THERE

Transit: Take TransLink Bus 209, 210 (Upper Lynn Valley), or 228 (Lynn Valley) to Underwood Avenue at Evelyn Street. Walk east via Evelyn Park (past the playground and tennis courts) and Evelyn Street, and cross Lynn Valley Road outside the Lynn Headwaters Regional Park gate. Descend Rice Lake Road, cross Pipeline Bridge, and ascend the gravel Footbridge Trail to reach the Rice Lake gate in 700 m (0.4 mi).

Vehicle: Westbound on Trans-Canada Highway 1 in North Vancouver, north of Ironworkers Memorial Second Narrows Crossing, take Exit 23B. Head east on Main Street, which becomes Dollarton Highway. Turn left on Riverside Drive, left on Mount Seymour Parkway, and right on Lillooet Road. (Eastbound on Highway 1, take Exit 21, go left on Keith Road, and turn left on Lillooet.) Drive 4.8 km (3 mi) farther, following Lillooet left at the Monashee Drive intersection and through the Lower Seymour Conservation Reserve gate. Fork right at road's end for the main parking lot (toilet available). Note the posted closing time, which can be as early as 5 p.m. in winter.

A rainy day at the Rice Lake Wharf.

THE HIKE

Locate the kiosk and benches at the north side of the parking lot, then go left past the washrooms to the Rice Lake gate and native plant garden. Briefly head north on the paved Seymour Valley Trailway, quickly bearing left onto the Lynn Headwaters Connector Trail. Pass picnic tables and Adirondack chairs and enter the woods.

Take the first gated trail on the right. Check out a recreated flume to see how loggers in the early 1900s transported shingle bolts (short sections of logs) stored in Rice Lake to Moodyville (Whua-hai-lum in həṅ̓q̓əmin̓əm̓, the language of the Tsleil-Waututh Nation). A historical sawmill company town on Burrard Inlet (Slílutulh to the Squamish Nation, Tsleil-Wat to the Tsleil-Waututh), Moodyville had a diverse labour force of African, Chinese, Chilean, First Nations, Kanaka (Hawaiian), and white workers. At a Rice Lake Wharf sign, turn right on the Rice Lake Loop Trail to begin a counterclockwise circumambulation of the lake.

Formerly known as Powell Lake, Rice Lake served as a City of North Vancouver drinking water reservoir, supplied by Lynn Creek (X̱a7élcha Swa7lt to the Squamish, Kan-ul-cha to the Tsleil-Waututh), from the 1920s to 1981. Pause to enjoy the view from the bench and viewing platform at the lakehead. Detour left by an outhouse to walk on the wharf, where the angling happens. A plaque commemorates Group of Seven

Sisters at the Rice Lake Wharf.

painter Frederick Varley (1881–1969), who lived on Rice Lake Road in the 1920s and '30s. Varley's watercolours from this period include *Bridge Over Lynn* and *The Trail to Rice Lake*.

Continue rounding the lake, keeping left on the main trail, crossing wooden bridges, and taking advantage of benches. Macrofungi spotted on deadwood include small stagshorn and summer oyster mushrooms. Ignore an exit to the Seymour Valley Trailway. An interpretive panel highlights the lake's contemporary outflow.

Where a trail to the Lynn Headwaters Connector goes straight ahead, turn left to finish circling the lake. Engraved boulders, off to the right at a bend, memorialize Trans-Canada Air Lines Flight 3, which disappeared in 1947 with 15 people aboard on its approach to Vancouver from Lethbridge, Alberta. The wreckage was discovered west of Mount Elsay in 1994. Go straight through the wharf junction to return to the Lynn Headwaters Connector, where you turn left and retrace your steps to the trailhead.

Established in 1987 and originally known as the Seymour Demonstration Forest, the Lower Seymour Conservation Reserve lies in the territories of the Musqueam, Squamish, and Tsleil-Waututh First Nations. No camping, drones, fires, flower or mushroom picking, smoking, or vaping. Bikes, boats, dogs, horses, inflatables, and swimming are prohibited at Rice Lake.

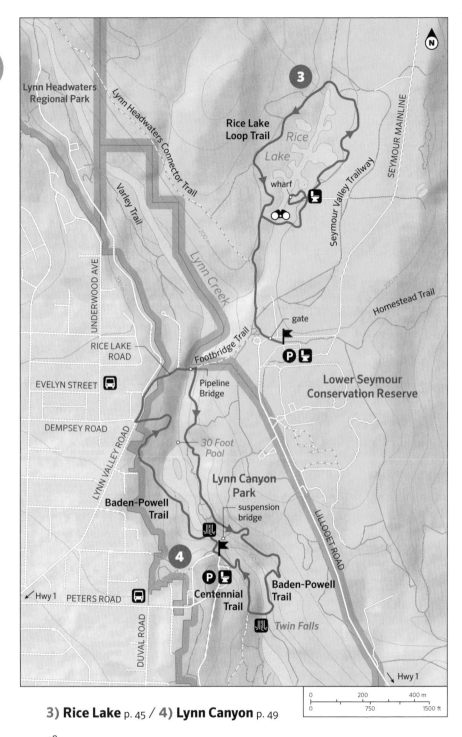

3) Rice Lake p. 45 / **4) Lynn Canyon** p. 49

4 Lynn Canyon

Distance: 3 km (1.9 mi)
Elevation gain: 170 m (560 ft)
High point: 260 m (850 ft)
Season: all year

Difficulty: ■
Quality: ☺ ☺ ☺
Map: Trail Ventures BC North Shore
Trailhead: 49°20'37" N, 123°01'07" W

LYNN CANYON in North Vancouver is a favourite hiking spot of many local kids, including my own. The free suspension bridge is the big draw. So are the plunging waterfalls, deep malachite-green pools, and tall conifers. Après-hike plans? The exhibits at the Lynn Canyon Ecology Centre and ice cream treats at the Lynn Canyon Café have you covered. The ease of access and sundry attractions will have you visiting again and again.

GETTING THERE

Transit: Take TransLink Bus 227 (Lynn Valley Centre) to Peters Road at Duval Road, or Bus 228 (Lynn Valley) to Lynn Valley Road at Peters Road. Walk east on Peters to Lynn Canyon Park.

Vehicle: On Trans-Canada Highway 1 in North Vancouver, take Exit 19 and head north on Lynn Valley Road. (Alternatively, from Exit 21, go north on Mountain Highway and turn right on Lynn Valley Road.) Turn right on Peters Road, 850 m (0.5 mi) past Mountain Highway. Enter Lynn Canyon Park (toilet available) in 700 m (0.4 mi). Find a space in one of the parking lots or, if they're full, legal street parking nearby. Note the park's posted closing time.

THE HIKE

The Lynn Canyon Suspension Bridge makes it possible to divide this hike into upper and lower loops—Pipeline Bridge (2 km/1.2 mi) and Twin Falls (1 km/0.6 mi). Nonetheless, the grand tour of the canyon, described in a clockwise direction, is well worthwhile.

Excitement at the Lynn Canyon Suspension Bridge.

Head toward the suspension bridge. Several signs warn of the hazards of cliff jumping, rock climbing, and swimming in the canyon, which has seen many deaths and injuries. Descend wooden stairs. Just before the bridge, turn left and go down more stairs, following a section of the Lynn Valley Link and Baden-Powell Trail (B-P Trail). Check out the top of a waterfall at the 90 Foot Pool, safely behind a chain-link fence.

Cross a bridge over a stream, with a beautiful view of Lynn Creek (X̱a7élcha Swa7lt to the Squamish Nation, Kan-ul-cha to the Tsleil-Waututh Nation). At a signpost, detour right to visit the creek's right bank. Potential wildlife sightings include American dippers, Columbian black-tailed deer, northern flying squirrels, Pacific banana slugs, and western red-backed salamanders. Follow the wide path through mud, over boardwalks, and up the stairs to Lynn Valley Road, opposite the End of the Line General Store, after 900 m (0.6 mi) on foot.

Turn right and, in one block, bear right onto Rice Lake Road. Descend to Pipeline Bridge (49°20′59″ N, 123°01′12″ W) and cross Lynn Creek to river left at the head of the canyon. Briefly head up the gravel Footbridge Trail and go right at the Lynn Canyon Park map. Head downstream on the wide path, pulling alongside a safety fence, amid tall Douglas-firs and big nurse stumps. Go straight through a junction onto a boardwalk with railings.

Descend eleventy or so wooden stairs to the 30 Foot Pool, which is often mobbed on hot summer days. Follow the broad, braided path downstream for 500 m (0.3 mi) to the east end of the Lynn Canyon Suspension Bridge. Along the way, kids can't resist scampering up a huge boulder. Take the steps left and away from the fence. To save Twin Falls for another day, cross the suspension bridge.

Otherwise, take the boardwalk on the left for the least-busy, most-beautiful rainforest section of our grand tour. Back on the B-P Trail, indicated by triangular fleur-de-lis markers, tread on long boardwalks with benches. Descend steps to the Twin Falls Bridge (49°20′29″ N, 123°00′57″ W), 600 m (0.4 mi) from the suspension bridge.

Immediately downstream, Lynn Creek thunders over two tiers, with a cave beside the lower plunge pool. Beginning in 1863, a box flume carried water from Twin Falls to Moodyville (Whua-hai-lum to the Tsleil-Waututh) on Burrard Inlet (Slílutulh to the Squamish, Tsleil-Wat to the Tsleil-Waututh) to power the first sawmill at the colonial settlement. These days, whitewater kayakers running Lynn Canyon (Class IV [advanced] at high water) typically put in at or below the waterfall.

Cross to river right, where an interpretive panel describes the life cycle of Pacific salmon, well known to schoolchildren in B.C. Tackle the stairs of the Centennial Trail. Turn right on a gravel road, which becomes a path along the fence atop the canyon rim, and head upstream to the café, washrooms, and ranger station. If you haven't ventured onto the suspension bridge yet, do it now.

Administered by the District of North Vancouver, Lynn Canyon Park lies in the territories of the Musqueam, Squamish, and Tsleil-Waututh First Nations. No camping, fires, fishing, littering, mountain biking, smoking, or vaping. Dogs must be leashed.

·················· **Fun Fact** ······················
The Lynn Canyon Suspension Bridge cost 10 cents to cross when it opened in 1912. That's around $3 in today's dollars.

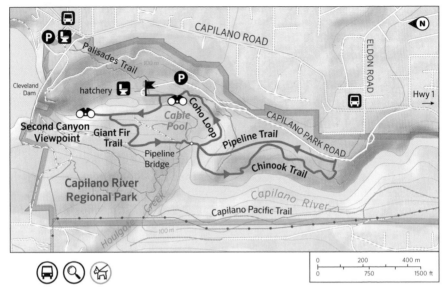

Distance: 4.1 km (2.5 mi)
Elevation gain: 60 m (200 ft)
High point: 115 m (380 ft)
Season: all year

Difficulty: ●
Quality: ☺ ☺ ☺
Map: Trail Ventures BC North Shore
Trailhead: 49°21′21″ N, 123°06′38″ W

CAPILANO RIVER REGIONAL PARK is worth repeat visits just to see salmon jumping at the Capilano River Hatchery and water gushing over the Cleveland Dam. Another big reason to take kids to Capilano Canyon is for a tour of the majestic old-growth trees.

GETTING THERE

Transit: Take TransLink Bus 232, 236, or 247 (Grouse Mountain) to Nancy Greene Way at Prospect Avenue. From the Capilano River Regional Park entrance, across the road, follow the Palisades Trail downstream to the Capilano River Hatchery.

Vehicle: On Trans-Canada Highway 1 in North Vancouver, take Exit 14. Head north on Capilano Road for 1.3 km (0.8 mi), passing Capilano Suspension Bridge Park. Turn left on Capilano Park Road, following signs for the Capilano River Hatchery (4500 Capilano Park Road; toilet available). Pull into the farthest parking lot that isn't full. Note the gate's posted closing time, which can be as early as 5 p.m. in winter.

THE HIKE

First things first—marvel at the giant Douglas-fir towering high above the other conifers at the foot of the main parking lot. At 76.5 m (251 ft), it's one of the tallest trees in Metro Vancouver.

Find the kiosk across the turnaround from the Capilano River Hatchery entrance. Follow a gravel path under an old, leaning Pacific yew, with purple underbark—bypassing the picnic shelter and tables to the left. Quickly, go right and take the Cable Pool Bridge over the Capilano River (xʷməθkʷəy̓əma?ɬ to the Musqueam Nation, Xwemélch'stn Stáḵw to the Squamish Nation).

Turn right and keep right to reach the often-misty Second Canyon Viewpoint, 500 m (0.3 mi) from the trailhead. The wooden viewing platform overlooks Ring Bolt Pool, guarded by sheer cliffs, at the foot of the 90-m (295-ft) tall Cleveland Dam. Interpretive panels shed light on the ecology, geomorphology, and history of the canyon.

Backtrack to the last junction—passing a lovely quote from *Legends of Vancouver* by Mohawk poet E. Pauline Johnson (Tekahionwake)—and turn right on the Giant Fir Trail, a link in the Trans Canada Trail (now known as the Great Trail). Head up the stairs and crane your neck at a pair of huge Douglas-firs, protected by a fence from damaging footsteps. Where stairs drop down to the left, go right to say hello to Grandfather Capilano, a 61-m (200-ft) high Douglas-fir that's the reason why my son calls all old-growth conifers "grandpa trees."

Continue up the stairs and make a left on a service road. Go right at the bottom, following signs to the Coho Loop. Keep left and right at subsequent junctions. Follow the fence to Pipeline Bridge and cross to river left. A bench offers a spot to pull out the chocolate-covered blueberries.

At a three-way junction just up the trail, turn right on the Chinook Trail. Scamper up a ruggedly steep bit to a level section. Clasping twistedstalk, deer fern, Oregon grape, salmonberry, and vine maple grow in the understory. Descend wooden steps, with a little bench at the top. Keep left at an unmarked fork and then right where the Chinook and Pipeline Trails almost merge. Cross a bridge over a brook.

Turn left on the Pipeline Trail, at a junction with a yellow gate (49°20′54″ N, 123°06′52″ W), 2 km (1.2 mi) from the Second Canyon Viewpoint. Pass Camp Capilano and a right-hand trail to Capilano Park Road. As you descend on loose gravel, spot Pipeline Bridge ahead. After 700 m (0.4 mi) on the Pipeline Trail, make a hard-right turn on the Coho Loop to stay on river left, with 900 m (0.6 mi) to go to the trailhead.

Stay right at an unsigned fork above Dog Leg Pool. Cross a bridge and go up steps. Notice the soil horizons exposed by the dramatically eroded cut slope. Keep left to reach a viewing platform, where you can watch folks fishing at Cable Pool. Bypass Cable Pool Bridge and go by the picnic shelter to return to the trailhead.

Before or after your hike, a visit to the Capilano River Hatchery, operated by Fisheries and Oceans Canada, is a must. You might see whitewater kayakers entering the Class III (intermediate) rapids immediately downstream. Check out the wooden mushroom bench by the Palisades Trail at the end of Capilano Park Road for a fun photo op.

Administered by Metro Vancouver, Capilano River Regional Park lies in the territories of the Musqueam, Squamish, and Tsleil-Waututh First Nations. No camping, drones, fires, flower or mushroom picking, mountain biking, smoking or vaping (except in designated areas), swimming, or wading. Dogs must be leashed on most trails.

·························· **Fun Fact** ·······················
Depending on the kind of fish you want to see, the best time of year to visit the Capilano River Hatchery is October to November (chinook salmon), June to November (coho salmon), or March to April (steelhead trout). Watch spawning adults make their way up the fish ladder or try to jump over the weir.

6 Cypress Falls

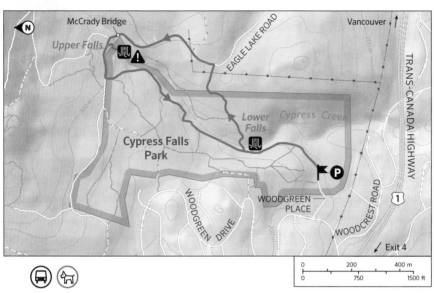

Distance: 3 km (1.9 mi)
Elevation gain: 120 m (390 ft)
High point: 310 m (1,020 ft)
Season: all year

Difficulty: ■
Quality: ☺ ☺
Map: Trail Ventures BC North Shore
Trailhead: 49°21'08" N, 123°14'27" W

MOST METRO VANCOUVERITES are familiar with Cypress Mountain—the ski area in West Vancouver, that is, not the minor summit in Coquitlam. Mention nearby Cypress Falls Park in most company, though, and you'll receive blank stares. Yes, the canyon of Cypress Creek (Stḵ'iil in Sḵwx̱wú7mesh sníchim, the language of the Squamish Nation) isn't as famous as a few of its North Shore counterparts, but it's well worth repeat visits with kids.

GETTING THERE

Transit: From Park Royal, take TransLink Bus 253 (Caulfeild) to Woodgreen Drive at Woodgreen Place. Walk east on Woodgreen Place to the park entrance.

Vehicle: On Trans-Canada Highway 1 in West Vancouver, take Exit 4. Follow signs for Woodgreen Drive. (From the westbound exit, go right.) Turn right on Woodgreen Place, 350 m (0.2 mi) past the westbound off-ramp. Go by the tennis courts and pull into the gravel parking lot at Cypress Falls Park.

THE HIKE

If the kids are in need of motivation, tell them Cypress Falls is a lollipop hike. (Well, it's true!) Head past the waste bins, through the grass, and into the woods. Go left and up at the first junction. Stick to main trails, following orange diamonds, except as noted. Side paths are numerous; some lead to cliffs and hazardous terrain. Keep kids close at all waterfall viewpoints.

In short order, the lower falls are found to the right of the trail. Cypress Creek flows through a slot in the rock and flies into the gorge below. Before you arrive at a fenced viewpoint on a slippery-when-wet outcrop above the falls, a side path on the right leads to a less obvious but more dramatic spot (also fenced) offering a perspective from downstream.

Continue up the trail and cross to river left on a wooden bridge, commencing a counterclockwise loop. Follow the heavily braided, rocky, and rooty path—beneath old-growth firs—up and away from Cypress Creek. Bear right where an orange marker is affixed to a cedar ahead. Go through a gate in a British Pacific Properties fence and under B.C. Hydro power lines.

Emerge on Eagle Lake Road, opposite a quarry. Turn left and head uphill on pavement, passing the West Vancouver school district's works yard and Powerline Road. Curve left to go by the Cypress Substation. Pass the yellow gate ahead and continue on gravel. Cross Cypress Creek back to river right on McCrady Bridge. Take the left (gravel) fork. (Right goes to the Eagle Lake water treatment plant.)

At the blue mushroom posts, detour left for a steep path down to a precarious, unfenced viewpoint of the segmented upper falls. Be extremely cautious; hold on to kids. Don't follow the rough path farther downstream as it runs rather treacherously atop the cliffs. Return to the gravel road and continue descending momentarily.

Head left on a wide, bark-mulched path to re-enter the woods (49°21′36″ N, 123°14′07″ W). Take stone steps down to an unfenced

The upper falls in Cypress Falls Park.

viewpoint of the lower tier of the upper falls. Don't try to descend the dodgy slope to get a better but potentially fatal vantage. Follow the orange diamonds downstream. Look left to spot Knuckle Head, an over-hanging cliff that's home to rock-climbing routes such as Cypress Crack.

Re-enter Cypress Falls Park at a fence gate. Admire big, old, fire-scarred firs and listen to ravens cawing as you hike along the canyon rim. A burnt cedar snag beside the trail is hollowed out so it appears to be standing on two legs—photo op! Cross a bridge over a streamlet and scamper up roots and rocks. Return to familiar ground by the bridge upstream of the lower falls. Retrace your steps to the trailhead. So, what was that you said about lollipops?

Administered by the District of West Vancouver, Cypress Falls Park lies in the territories of the Musqueam, Squamish, and Tsleil-Waututh First Nations. The park provides habitat for the northern red-legged frog, a species of special concern. Archery, camping, drones, fires, littering, and smoking are prohibited. Dogs must be under control. Human companions should pick up dog waste and refrain from leaving poop bags beside the trail, even temporarily.

7 Lost Lake

[Map: Cypress Provincial Park area showing Nordic Ski Area, downhill ski area, Burfield Trail, Baden-Powell Trail, West Lake Trail, Sitzmark Trail, First Lake, West Lake, Hollyburn Lodge, Marr Creek, Stoney Creek, Brothers Creek, Blue Gentian L., Lost Lake Trail, Lost Lake, Cypress Bowl Road, Hwy 1]

Distance: 8.5 km (5.3 mi)
Elevation gain: 180 m (590 ft)
High point: 940 m (3,080 ft)
Season: late spring to early fall

Difficulty: ◆
Quality: ☺ ☺
Map: Friends of Cypress Provincial Park Southern Section
Trailhead: 49°22′45″ N, 123°11′30″ W

FOUR LAKES, ONE HIKE—let's call this sweet deal on Hollyburn Mountain the family pack. Enjoy the novelty of strolling through the cross-country ski area (for free) in the off-season, take a dip in a lake or two, and hunt for slime moulds in the forest. Lost Lake in Cypress Provincial Park is a fine destination for both sunny and rainy days.

GETTING THERE

Vehicle: On Trans-Canada Highway 1 in West Vancouver, take Exit 8. Continue onto Cypress Bowl Road and head up to Cypress Provincial Park. In 13.5 km (8.4 mi), turn right and pull into the parking lot at the base of the Nordic ski area (toilet available).

THE HIKE

Lost Lake can be reached from the top of the silk-stocking British Properties, but starting at the Nordic ski area makes for a more leisurely hike with less elevation gain. From the B.C. Parks kiosk on the east side of the parking lot, before the resort buildings, head under the power lines. Quickly turn left on the access road (also known as Lower Powerline), then right on the Burfield Trail, an easy run for cross-country skiers in winter.

Fork left, where Ski School Flats goes right. Pass Sidewinder (left) and an outhouse (right). Go straight through a junction with Lower Telemark and Short Cut. Keep right at Zig Zag to arrive between First Lake and the Hollyburn Lodge in 850 m (0.5 mi). In 2017, the Hollyburn Heritage Society celebrated the opening of the rebuilt lodge. The historic ski camp here originally opened in 1927.

Go forth, passing a picnic table and an old ranger station and crossing the Nasmyth Bridge over the lake's outlet to Marr Creek. Stay on the road, where a boardwalk exits to the right, then transfer from Sitzmark to Grand National. Pass a cabin called The Doghouse. Fork left onto Jack Pratt and go by the remains of a 1958 ski jump. Follow the road straight across ski trails and onto the West Lake run. Fork right after an old boardwalk.

Reach a signpost (49°22′39″ N, 123°10′19″ W) indicating the trail to Lost Lake goes right, 1.4 km (0.9 mi) past the Hollyburn Lodge. First, go forward several steps to check out the old dam on West Lake, a wonderful swimming hole surrounded by forest. Head southeast on a rooty

Fog at Blue Gentian Lake.

path, paralleling the canyon of Stoney Creek. Cross a bridge over a tributary and go left.

At the next junction, detour right to visit muddy Blue Gentian Lake (49°22'31" N, 123°09'59" W), formerly known as Middle Lake, 650 m (0.4 mi) from West Lake. Amble left (where there's a picnic table) or right on the boardwalk to enjoy the wetland flora, particularly the king gentians, if they are in bloom. (Turn around here for a shorter hike of intermediate difficulty.)

Keep going 1.3 km (0.8 mi) farther, north then east, on the rougher Lost Lake Trail. Kids may need help boulder-hopping Stoney Creek and Brothers Creek, due to their steep banks. Tread carefully over slippery rocks and roots, mud puddles, and deadfall. Finally, fork left to reach the shore of Lost Lake (49°22'32" N, 123°09'28" W), formerly known as East Lake. Eye the water for amphibians and aquatic insects, and contemplate a dip.

Retracing your steps to the trailhead is the simplest, most scenic option. Save enough energy—most of the elevation gain is on the way back. Look for wolf's milk, a fungus-like plasmodial slime mould that's sometimes pink, on decaying wood. All four lakes drain to Burrard Inlet (Slílutulh to the Squamish Nation, Tsleil-Wat to the Tsleil-Waututh Nation).

Cypress Provincial Park lies in the territories of the Musqueam, Squamish, and Tsleil-Waututh First Nations. No drones, fires, flower or mushroom picking, mountain biking, smoking, or vaping. Dogs must be leashed. During the ski season, First Lake and West Lake are only accessible to paying customers of the Cypress Mountain resort.

···················· **Fun Fact** ·······················

In the early 1900s, loggers used flumes—a sort of V-shaped waterslide—to move shingle bolts (short sections of logs) from the slopes of Hollyburn Mountain to sawmills below. Taking a risk, people also rode the bolts down the flumes. If you've ever been on the log ride at an amusement park, including the Flume at the Pacific National Exhibition's Playland, you can imagine what that was like!

8 ◣ Bowen Lookout

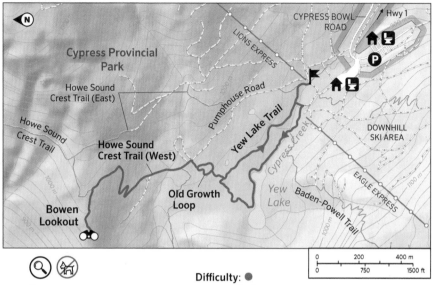

Distance: 4.3 km (2.7 mi)
Elevation gain: 120 m (390 ft)
High point: 1,030 m (3,380 ft)
Season: late spring to early fall

Difficulty: ●
Quality: ☺ ☺
Map: Friends of Cypress Provincial Park Southern Section
Trailhead: 49°23′49″ N, 123°12′15″ W

TAKE A STROLL in a subalpine wetland and learn all about these flooded ecosystems. Go higher to gaze upon one of North America's southernmost fjords. The hike to Bowen Lookout in Cypress Provincial Park offers plenty of intrigue for young aspiring hikers and their companions.

GETTING THERE

Vehicle: On Trans-Canada Highway 1 in West Vancouver, take Exit 8. Continue onto Cypress Bowl Road and drive 15 km (9.3 mi) up to the parking lots at the base of Cypress Provincial Park's downhill ski area (toilet and electric vehicle charging available).

THE HIKE

Our reverse lollipop hike follows the Yew Lake Trail, a barrier-free interpretive path, and the west branch of the Howe Sound Crest Trail (HSCT). Find the B.C. Parks kiosk, flanked by benches, past the Cypress Creek Lodge and Olympic rings (916 m/3,005 ft). From the signpost to the right, set off on the wide gravel surface of the Yew Lake Trail. Watch out for black bears!

Within the first 300 m (0.2 mi), fork left to spurn the east (old) branch of the HSCT, turn left and right at subsequent junctions, and encounter an interpretive panel about deer-cabbage. Next, the Baden-Powell Trail (also known as the Black Mountain Trail in winter) exits left.

Follow Cypress Creek (Stḵ'iil in Sḵwx̱wú7mesh sníchim, the language of the Squamish Nation) upstream to Yew Lake, formerly known as Cypress Lake, itself. Pause at picnic tables for open-water views and at panels to learn about yellow pond-lily, buckbean, glacial erratics, and peat bogs. Stay on the level trail to protect the wetland vegetation.

After 1 km (0.6 mi) on foot, reach a signposted junction. Going right would deliver you back to the trailhead in 700 m (0.4 mi). However, save the rest of the Yew Lake loop for the return, and turn left for the short Old Growth Loop. The wheelchair-accessible path splits and rejoins, so do one side now and the other later. Walk among several-centuries-old amabilis fir and mountain hemlock trees.

At the north end of the Old Growth Loop, turn left on the west branch of the HSCT (also known as the Bowen Lookout Trail in winter). The destination viewpoint is 1.1 km (0.7 mi) farther. Bear right to cross a bridge and begin gaining elevation. Alpine marsh and stream violets are plentiful, as is bunchberry.

Turn left at the next junction, with 240 m (260 yd) to go. (The HSCT continues north to St. Marks Summit and beyond on its 29-km [18-mi] journey to the Sea to Sky Highway, south of Porteau Cove [Xwáẃchayay].) Lose a bit of elevation on the way to the Bowen Lookout (49°24′23″ N, 123°12′49″ W), 2.3 km (1.4 mi) from the trailhead.

From the log bench and gravel pad, retained by interlocking concrete blocks, feast on the view of Bowen Island (č̓əw̓č̓əw̓ʔiqən̓ in the hən̓q̓əmin̓əm̓ language of the Musqueam Nation, Nex̱wlélex̱wem to the Squamish), Gambier Island (Cha7élḵnech to the Squamish), and Bowyer Island (Lháḵw'tich) in Howe Sound (Átl'ḵa7tsem). However, don't share your lunch with those bold Steller's jays.

Hiking on the Howe Sound Crest Trail.

Howe Sound (Átl'ḵa7tsem) from the Bowen Lookout.

When everyone's satisfied, begin the return to the trailhead. Be sure to complete the Old Growth Loop and Yew Lake Trail on the way back.

Cypress Provincial Park lies in the territories of the Musqueam, Squamish, and Tsleil-Waututh First Nations. Established in 1975, the park derives its name from the yellow cypress tree, which is also known as yellow, Alaska, or Nootka cedar. The word for this conifer in Sḵwx̱wú7mesh sníchim, the language of the Squamish Nation, is k'elhmáy̓. The Friends of Cypress Provincial Park Society advocates for public access to the park and the preservation of its natural, historical, and cultural features.

No drones, fires, flower or mushroom picking, mountain biking, smoking, or vaping. Dogs are prohibited on the Yew Lake Trail due to the sensitive environment. (Guide dogs for people with blindness or low vision are the exception.) In winter, snowshoers must pick up a free backcountry-access-corridor tag at the Black Mountain Lodge to pass through the Cypress Mountain ski area en route to the Bowen Lookout.

9 ▶ Erin Moore Trail | Photo on p. 27

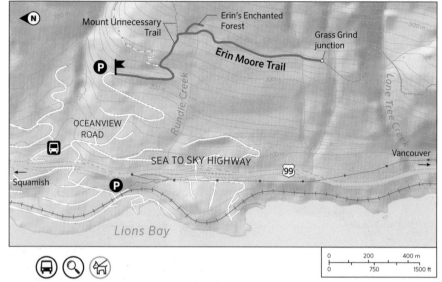

Distance: 3.2 km (2 mi)
Elevation gain: 155 m (510 ft)
High point: 360 m (1,180 ft)
Season: all year

Difficulty: ◆
Quality: ☺ ☺
Map: Trail Ventures BC North Shore
Trailhead: 49°27′22″ N, 123°13′50″ W

THE ERIN MOORE TRAIL traverses the lower slopes of Unnecessary Mountain in Lions Bay. Its focal point is a grove of old-growth trees dedicated to the memory of Erin Kate Moore (2007–2014), who died in a rockslide while hiking at nearby Lone Tree Creek (P'ap'k̲' in S̲k̲w̲x̲wú7mesh sníchim, the language of the Squamish Nation). Kids will enjoy discovering the myriad curiosities placed on the warren of paths in Erin's Enchanted Forest. Standing among all the ornaments, painted rocks, and prayer flags, you can't help but appreciate the family's and community's love for the trail's namesake.

GETTING THERE

Transit: Take TransLink Bus 262 (Brunswick) from Caulfeild Village or the Horseshoe Bay ferry terminal to Crosscreek Road at Centre Road. Head south on Crosscreek. Turn left on Oceanview Road and walk 1 km (0.6 mi) to the top.

Vehicle: On Highway 99 (Sea to Sky Highway), 12 km (7.5 mi) north of its junction with Trans-Canada Highway 1 at Horseshoe Bay, take the Lions Bay Avenue exit. From the northbound off-ramp, keep right to merge with Oceanview Road. (From the southbound off-ramp, keep left at Isleview Place, turn left on Lions Bay Avenue, and continue onto Oceanview.) Keep right at Crosscreek Road and drive to the top of Oceanview. A few parallel parking spots are available (in front of 395 Oceanview Road). Alternatively, find a legal parking spot lower down on Oceanview or pay parking at Lions Bay Beach Park.

THE HIKE

From the top of Oceanview Road, head up the gated access road into the Harvey Creek Community Watershed, which supplies potable water to Lions Bay. Pass a bench and a water tank. The road goes from pavement to gravel and then bends left.

In 400 m (0.2 mi), find the signed start of the Mount Unnecessary Trail on the right. Tackle the steep, rocky path, with the help of some log steps. Follow the beaded Es for 200 m (220 yd) to a key fork with directional signs on a log. Left eventually leads to the Howe Sound Crest Trail and the summit of Unnecessary Mountain (1,548 m/5,080 ft). However, go right to begin the Erin Moore Trail.

Turn right where an Unnecessary Mountain arrow points left on a sawed-off log. Head past angel, bird, and butterfly ornaments and tall Douglas-fir and western red cedar trees. At the next junction (49°27′11″ N, 123°13′40″ W), a wooden sign indicates Erin's Enchanted Forest lies off to the left. Painted rocks lie at the base of a tree with a wreath and a rainbow heart on its trunk.

Explore the small web of paths leading to a memorial sign next to Rundle Creek. There's an Easter egg banner, hearts, a plush snake, wind chimes, and many more knick-knacks scattered about these woods. Return to the entrance of Erin's Enchanted Forest. A little visit to the grove will satisfy many kids, but it's worth continuing south on the Erin Moore Trail to enjoy the woods in a more natural state.

Beyond Erin's Enchanted Forest, the trail is rougher, muddy, and rooty, and marked only by rare pink flagging. Nevertheless, the majestic old-growth cedars and firs (one positively dripping with sap), huge stumps, and mossy logs make it a rewarding foray. Turn around at a junction with the stiff Grass Grind (49°26′49″ N, 123°13′46″ W), 800 m (2,625 ft) from Erin's Enchanted Forest, and retrace your steps to Oceanview Road.

The rest of the Erin Moore Trail is not recommended for young kids or inexperienced hikers. From the Grass Grind junction, the rugged path veers sharply uphill and then plunges into a wild ravine to cross Lone Tree Creek. The path leads to a bluff overlooking Howe Sound (Átl'ḵa7tsem to the Squamish Nation) and Bowen Island (ċəẃċəẃʔiqən in the hən̓q̓əmin̓əm̓ language of the Musqueam Nation, Nex̱wlélex̱wem to the Squamish), before continuing upslope and looping back to the Mount Unnecessary Trail higher up the mountain.

The Erin Moore Trail lies in the territories of the Musqueam and Squamish First Nations. Amplified music and smoking are prohibited on Lions Bay trails. Dogs must be leashed and poop cleaned up. Please note: The Erin Moore Trail is a special case; in general, it is not appropriate to place memorials, painted rocks, and tree ornaments in the backcountry.

····················· **Fun Fact** ·····················

A forest on the B.C. coast that has trees older than 250 years is called "old growth." In the Interior, a tree must be older than 140 years. For reference, Canada wasn't yet a country 250 years ago. And 140 years ago, the Canadian Pacific Railway was just being built.

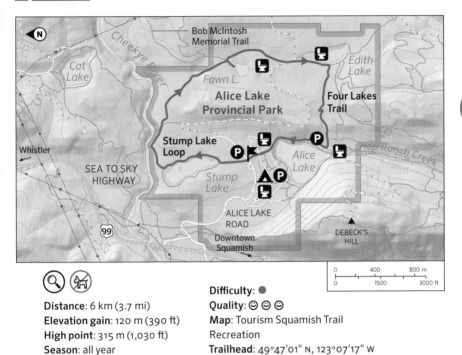

Distance: 6 km (3.7 mi)
Elevation gain: 120 m (390 ft)
High point: 315 m (1,030 ft)
Season: all year

Difficulty: ●
Quality: ☺ ☺ ☺
Map: Tourism Squamish Trail Recreation
Trailhead: 49°47′01″ N, 123°07′17″ W

ALICE LAKE PROVINCIAL PARK in Squamish is an ideal environment for introducing children to the joys of camping (or glamping). The Four Lakes Trail is perfect for a first hike too. Going clockwise, the easy loop visits Stump, Fawn, Edith, and Alice Lakes. There are bald eagles to spot, mosses to feel, and bridges to tread. A playground is the last stop on this scenic tour of the much-visited park.

GETTING THERE

Vehicle: On Highway 99 (Sea to Sky Highway), 9.8 km (6.1 mi) north of Downtown Squamish, turn east on Alice Lake Road. Enter Alice Lake Provincial Park and take the left fork in 1.2 km (0.7 mi). Continue

500 m (0.3 mi), passing the sani-dump station, to find the Four Lakes Trail parking area on the left. (Toilet available in the campground.)

THE HIKE

Enter the shady forest behind the trailhead kiosk, opposite a campground gatehouse, and set off north on the Four Lakes Trail. The first fork comes in 300 m (0.2 mi). Go right for the east side of the Stump Lake Loop. The soft, wide path visits interpretive panels and lakeshore viewpoints. See a little island and the forest reflected in the water.

Where both sides of the Stump Lake Loop reunite, go right. Amble among old-growth trees and big stumps. Keep right as you near the Cheekye River, then switchback uphill and away.

Fork left for Fawn Lake at the next junction. Detour right at a signpost to check out the smallest of the four lakes (49°47′05″ N, 123°06′32″ W), at the halfway point of the loop. Back on the main trail, continue forward a few steps to a junction with the Bob McIntosh Memorial Trail; go right.

An island reflected in Stump Lake.

Fog at Alice Lake.

A sign calls the section ahead Toad Alley. In August, keep your eyes on the ground so you don't crush the fingernail-sized western toadlets that migrate across the road en masse. Pass by an outhouse and a boulder barrier, on your right. Cross a road diagonally. Arrive at a junction with a private road on the left; find a path to the shore of Edith Lake, the site of a logging camp in the 1920s and '30s, behind the outhouse.

Following signs for Alice Lake, go right at the next two junctions. Having saved the biggest lake for last, descend switchbacks. Cross and recross Chuckling Creek on wooden bridges in a pretty ravine. Reach a parking lot and descend steps to a swimming dock on Alice Lake. The lake drains via Hop Ranch Creek (Smálutsin in S̱ḵwx̱wú7mesh sníchim, the language of the Squamish Nation) to the Squamish River (S̱ḵwx̱wú7mesh Staḵw).

Turn right on the Alice Lake Trail, cross Chuckling Creek one more time (got any dad jokes?), and go by several picnic tables. Stay left at a fork, then take a path up to the right. Walk the road north through the campground—detour left for the playground, washrooms, and beach—to return to the trailhead.

Dogs are prohibited on the Alice Lake Trail, on beaches, and in picnic areas; pets must be leashed elsewhere in Alice Lake Provincial Park. No littering, flower or mushroom picking, smoking, or vaping. Popular with trail runners (and the location of one of the 5 Peaks trail races), the Four Lakes Trail is closed to mountain biking between May 1 and September 15; the Edith Lake–Alice Lake section is bike-free year-round.

Distance: 3.5 km (2.2 mi)
Elevation gain: 40 m (130 ft)
High point: 310 m (1,020 ft)
Season: all year

Difficulty: ■
Quality: ☺ ☺
Map: NTS 92-G/14 Cheakamus River
Trailhead: 49°49'20" N, 123°08'01" W

A ROADSIDE oasis in Squamish, Brohm Lake draws hikers, trail runners, canoeists, stand-up paddleboarders, swimmers, cliff jumpers, birders, fishers, and picnickers to its shores. It's the centrepiece of Brohm Lake Interpretive Forest, which boasts an excellent network of family-friendly trails. Hit the Brohm Lake Trail to saunter beneath towering trees and savour clifftop views.

GETTING THERE
Vehicle: On Highway 99 (Sea to Sky Highway), 14.5 km (9 mi) north of Downtown Squamish, turn east into the Brohm Lake Interpretive Forest parking lot (toilet available).

THE HIKE
Brohm Lake is an expansion of Brohm Creek, the west fork of the Brohm River (Syexwáy̓akalh in Sḵwx̱wú7mesh sníchim, the language of the Squamish Nation), a tributary of the Cheekye River. Our counterclockwise loop sticks with the wide, undulating Brohm Lake Trail, which is mostly hiking-only, all the way around the lake.

Start by the kiosk at the north end of the parking lot, and head right into the woods. Quickly fork right and pass the outhouses. Read a couple of interpretive signs describing some of the plants and fungi you'll see on the trail, such as cattail, kinnikinnick, maiden-hair fern, and skunk cabbage.

In 200 m (220 yd), keep right to bypass the Rock Bluff Loop. Enjoy the calming sights of moss-capped outcrops and tall Douglas-fir trees. A fence guards a drop-off before a sublime blufftop viewpoint presents itself off to the left. Keep kids close on the slippery rock. A stone memorial provides a tragic example of the dangers of cliff jumping.

Head up beautiful wooden staircases fronting a rock face. Descend to meet the Powerline Trail, which follows a B.C. Hydro right-of-way, 500 m (0.3 mi) from the previous junction. Go left and descend steps and the path beside a steep creek amid western red cedars and below mossy cliffs. Take a lovely bridge over the steep creek. Drop down two more flights of stairs to lake level. Roots and rocks make the path slower going for the less sure-footed. An old-growth cedar leans over deep, clear Brohm Creek, which is crossed on a bridge.

Go left at the Brohm Creek Trail junction, 400 m (0.2 mi) after the Powerline Trail. In 100 m (110 yd), keep left at the Thompson Trail, which goes to the Tenderfoot Creek Hatchery. Head south for 800 m (0.5 mi), communing with old-growth survivors of railway and truck logging in the mid-1900s, on the quieter west side of the lake. Stay right at an unsigned junction and then left at the Connector Trail, which offers access to an old fire lookout via the steep Tantalus View Trail.

Meet the Bridge Trail in 1 km (0.6 mi). Go left to cross the bridge over the wetland at the foot of the lake. Turn left on the other side. Head 500 m (0.3 mi) north, next to the Sea to Sky Highway, passing a rocky viewpoint and arriving at the kiosk and outhouse at the south end of the parking lot.

The provincial recreation site at Brohm Lake was established in 1974 and the lake trail built in 1983. Camping, littering, and shooting are prohibited. Dogs must be leashed and poop picked up. Get there early on hot days before the parking lot fills up. Shoulder parking is prohibited on Highway 99.

··················· **Fun Fact** ···················

Although it is best known for its stinky smell and bright yellow flowers, skunk cabbage (also known as the Skeena lily or swamp lantern) is a food. If you cook them properly, you can eat the roots. Indigenous medicine uses skunk cabbage leaves to treat burns.

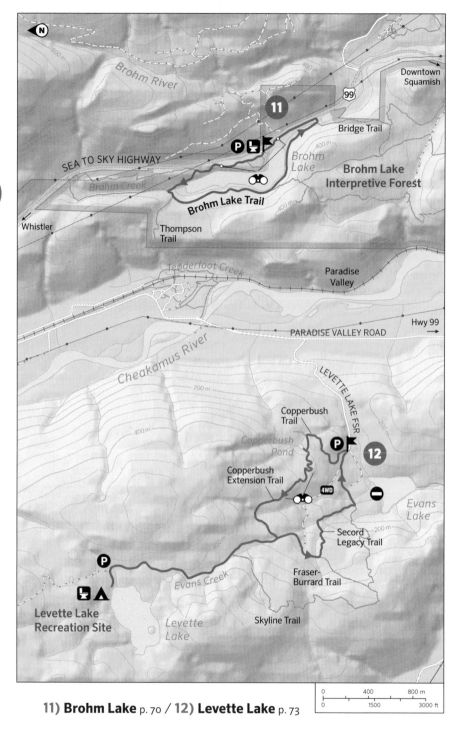

11) Brohm Lake p. 70 / **12) Levette Lake** p. 73

12 Levette Lake

Distance: 8 km (5 mi)
Elevation gain: 300 m (985 ft)
High point: 430 m (1,410 ft)
Season: most of the year

Difficulty: ◆
Quality: ☺ ☺ ☺
Map: NTS 92-G/14 Cheakamus River
Trailhead: 49°48'55" N, 123°10'07" W

THE WOODS around Evans Lake (Sa7aḿúy̓shn in Sḵwx̱wú7mesh sníchim, the language of the Squamish Nation) are full of nostalgia for those of us who spent time during our formative years at the outdoor education camp in the Paradise Valley area. Our reverse lollipop hike samples the quiet trails trodden by young campers over the years, pays off with a stunning view at Levette Lake, and passes by the rustic camp itself.

GETTING THERE

Vehicle: On Highway 99 (Sea to Sky Highway), 9.8 km (6.1 mi) north of Downtown Squamish, turn west on Squamish Valley Road (across from Alice Lake Provincial Park). In 3.7 km (2.3 mi), after crossing Fergie's Bridge over the Cheakamus River, go right on Paradise Valley Road for 2.3 km (1.4 mi). Across from the Cheakamus Centre, turn left on Levette Lake Forest Service Road, which turns to gravel (2WD). Find the tiny Copperbush Trail parking area on the right, 1.5 km (0.9 mi) up the logging road, opposite the Evans Lake Forest Education Centre gate and a sewage disposal site.

THE HIKE

Start up the old rocky roadbed, left of the kiosk, on the Copperbush Trail. It's a self-guided interpretive walk, but the pamphlets are typically missing in action at the trailhead. In 600 m (0.4 mi), turn left on a lush forest path. (Keep right at the junction for the brief scramble to Silver Summit, a sleepout site for the Evans Lake camp.) Pass little reflecting pools and detour right at a wooden arrow to view Copperbush Pond from the rotting remains of a shelter.

The Tantalus Range (Tsewílx̱)
behind Levette Lake.

Continue west on the Copperbush Extension Trail, which is marked with red-painted can lids and orange metal triangles. The delightful single track leads up and along mossy outcrops and through conifers draped in witch's hair. Earn a partial view south to Mount Habrich and Sky Pilot Mountain. The ridge path calls for big steps up and down and a sure foot on slippery rocks.

A better viewpoint faces southwest toward Omega Mountain (Nexwyúx̱wm) and the Tantalus Range (Tsewílx̱). Follow the path onto an old logging road. Ghost pipe, found here, resembles a fungus. Interestingly, this white flower is actually a non-photosynthetic, myco-heterotrophic plant that parasitizes mushrooms.

Descend to a creek, cross the bridge, and turn right to head up Levette Lake FSR, after 2.3 km (1.4 mi) on foot. Salmonberries, thimbleberries, and common foxglove, a European invasive species, offer a distraction from the road walking. Watch out for 4×4 vehicles. Ignore two private roads on the left. Past power pole 35, cross a bridge, and turn right before the road goes up a steep incline.

Enter the Levette Lake Recreation Site (49°50′02″ N, 123°11′03″ W), 4.2 km (2.6 mi) from the trailhead. It's a popular place for camping (first come, first served), swimming, canoeing, and stand-up paddleboarding. Go by pit toilets and food caches, look for signs indicating the designated day-use areas between campsites, and pick a spot on the lakeshore for lunch. The view is magnificent and likely to induce cabin envy. Snow-capped Omega Mountain, Mount Pelops, Mount Niobe, Alpha Mountain (Ḵiyáy̓aḵep), Mount Dione, and Mount Tantalus dominate across the water. Labrador tea grows on shore.

Head back down Levette Lake FSR to start the 4-km (2.5-mi) return route. Pass the Skyline Trail (right) after power pole 21 and the Copperbush Extension Trail (left) before pole 15. Just past pole 11, find an overgrown trail entrance on the right at a leftward bend in the road. Follow the Fraser-Burrard Trail into the woods.

In short order, turn left on the Secord Legacy Trail, which is indicated by can lids painted with the initials "LS." Take the soft path across a creek and through salal and deadfall. Cross the Evans Creek bridge. Turn right at a junction with blue flagging and black can lids. The Secord Legacy Trail ends at the Evans Lake Forest Education Centre's campfire circle.

Go left for the exit trail. Respect signage asking hikers to stay on the path; Evans Lake and the camp's grounds are off-limits to the public. Pass a huge Douglas-fir, fork left before the cabins, and continue to Levette Lake FSR. A right turn delivers you back to the trailhead.

The Evans Lake Forest Education Centre dates back to 1960, when a Junior Forest Wardens camp relocated from Point Atkinson (Sḵ'íw̓itsut) in West Vancouver. I have fond memories of attending the camp in the 1990s with my class from Harbour View Elementary School in Coquitlam. (The girls raided our cabin and hoisted my underpants up the flagpole. Sadly, a teacher cancelled the night's dance in the ensuing uproar.)

Camping, fires, flower picking, motorized vehicles, shooting, and smoking are prohibited in the Evans Lake Forest Education Society–managed demonstration forest. The Levette Lake Recreation Site is an amplified-sound-free zone.

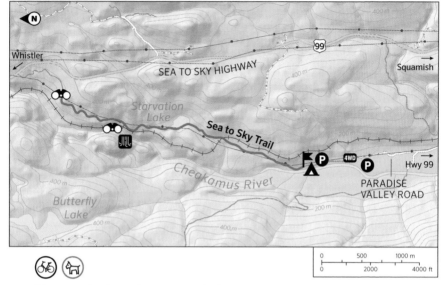

Distance: 7 km (4.3 mi)
Elevation gain: 235 m (770 ft)
High point: 330 m (1,080 ft)
Season: most of the year

Difficulty: ■
Quality: ☺ ☺
Map: NTS 92-G/14 Cheakamus River
Trailhead: 49°53'24" N, 123°10'52" W

MAKE A SPLASH at Starvation Lake. Chase trains in the dramatic setting of Cheakamus Canyon. Take a hike on the Sea to Sky Trail (An esxwéxwkw shewálh in S$\underline{k}$w$\underline{x}$wú7mesh sníchim, the language of the Squamish Nation), north of Squamish, and do both. Make sure to bring plenty of food and water though. You don't want the kids to remember Starvation Lake for the wrong reasons.

GETTING THERE

Vehicle: On Highway 99 (Sea to Sky Highway), 9.8 km (6.1 mi) north of Downtown Squamish, turn west on Squamish Valley Road (across from Alice Lake Provincial Park). In 3.7 km (2.3 mi), after crossing Fergie's Bridge over the Cheakamus River, go right on Paradise

Valley Road. Head north on pavement and then gravel. Join a power-line corridor, cross Culliton Creek, negotiate potholes, and arrive at big turn-around—the 2WD parking area (49°53′00″ N, 123°10′44″ W)—14 km (8.7 mi) from the highway. With 4WD and high clearance, continue 800 m (0.5 mi) farther to the camping area at the very muddy road's end. Note: This road is prone to flooding.

THE HIKE

Find the Sea to Sky Trail sign and boulder blockade at the north end of Paradise Valley Road. The left bank of the Cheakamus River (Ch'iyákmesh Stakw in Skwxwú7mesh sníchim) is immediately accessible. However, keep kids out of the swift glacial milk. Follow the roadbed upstream—if it's flooded, a path bypasses this section on the right—then away from the river. Watch out for mountain bikers.

Pass an overgrown red gate under a high-voltage power line. The wide path cuts across boulder slopes. Blackberry, hardhack, oceanspray, saskatoon, and thimbleberry shrubs soak up the sun. Shade is at a premium here, so a cloudy day is preferable unless you plan to take a lake dip. Clamber over boulders and carefully cross the Canadian National Railway track.

Arrive at the west shore of Starvation Lake (49°54′11″ N, 123°10′26″ W), which boasts dragonflies, lily pads, and relatively warm water, 1.7 km (1.1 mi) from the trailhead. (Turn back here for a shorter, beginner-level hike.) At the lakehead, fork left to stay on the Sea to Sky Trail and resume rising under the power line. You're tracing an old pack route, the 1877 Lillooet–Burrard Inlet Trail (also known as the Pemberton Trail), which itself followed a First Nations trade route. Start seeing railway tunnels and bridges and whitewater below in Cheakamus Canyon.

At 2.7 km (1.7 km), the trail slices across a rock face in exhilarating fashion. Tread on wire mesh, with nothing else but air below your feet. If the kids are acrophobic, you'll know now. The cliff to your left is draped with rockfall netting. A waterfall soon enters the picture. A viewpoint atop mossy boulder slopes, 3.3 km (2.1 mi) in, offers a look back down the narrow gorge, with a backdrop of the Tantalus Range (Tsewílx), including Omega Mountain (Nexwyúxwm) and Alpha Mountain (Kiyáyakep).

Push on a wee bit farther to earn a spectacular upstream view from a rock beside the trail (49°55′01″ N, 123°10′11″ W). Keep kids away from

A Canadian National Railway bridge on the Cheakamus River (Ch'iyákmesh Stakw).

the edge. Marvel at the rail bridge in the depths of the canyon, and spot where the Sea to Sky Trail emerges by a southbound pullout (an alternative starting point) on the Sea to Sky Highway. Turn around here for a pleasant descent to Paradise Valley Road, 3.5 km (2.2 mi) away.

The Sea to Sky Trail will eventually link Squamish and D'Arcy—via Whistler, Pemberton, and Mount Currie—with a 180-km (110-mi) route for self-propelled travel. It's part of the Trans Canada Trail system. No horses or motorized vehicles.

Fun Fact

The Trans Canada Trail (renamed the Great Trail of Canada between 2016 and 2021) is a network of land and water routes that cover 27,000 km (17,000 mi) in 13 provinces and territories. That's farther than circling the whole of Mars (21,297 km/13,233 mi).

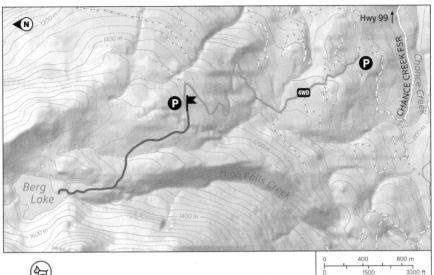

Distance: 3.9 km (2.4 mi)
Elevation gain: 140 m (460 ft)
High point: 1,510 m (4,950 ft)
Season: summer

Difficulty: ◆
Quality: ☺ ☺ ☺
Map: NTS 92-G/14 Cheakamus River
Trailhead: 49°59′12″ N, 123°13′27″ W

BERG LAKE is a remote alpine gem lying at the foot of Tricouni Peak (2,122 m/6,960 ft) and the headwaters of High Falls Creek (Skawshn in Sḵwx̱wú7mesh sníchim, the language of the Squamish Nation). Bask in the Coast Mountains, marvel at wildflower meadows, and whistle with hoary marmots on the trail. A rough 4×4 road is the price of admission.

GETTING THERE

Vehicle: On Highway 99 (Sea to Sky Highway), 31 km (19 mi) north of Downtown Squamish and 27 km (17 mi) south of Whistler Village, turn west on Chance Creek Forest Service Road. Cross the Cheakamus River and Canadian National Railway tracks. Bear left at a gated road and then right, away from the rails. The mainline bends left at a big yellow gate. Fork left, 3 km (1.9 mi) up the FSR, then keep right. Take the left fork after 5 km (3.1 mi). Fork right, before the 7-km (4.3-mi) marker. Pass a basalt column quarry. 2WD vehicles can make it as far as 8 km (5 mi), where a blocked spur lies ahead (940 m/3,080 ft; 49°58′15″ N, 123°12′59″ W). With 4WD and high clearance, bear right; it's 3.5 km (2.2 mi) farther to the trailhead. Take the next left fork. Go right on an overgrown road. (If you enter the quarry, you missed it.) Fork right and ford a creek. Continue up the steep and loose road, through big water bars, and park before a rock pile at road's end.

THE HIKE

Step outside and survey the volcanoes of Garibaldi Provincial Park on the eastern skyline: The Black Tusk (T'ekt'akmúy̓in tl'a In7inyáxa7en [Landing Place of the Thunderbird] in Skwxwú7mesh sníchim), Mount Price, and Mount Garibaldi (Nch'ḵay̓). From the rock pile (1,370 m/4,495 ft), continue west on the deteriorating roadbed in a clear-cut. Stay alert for black and grizzly bears!

Berg Lake with Cloudburst Mountain (Saẁpa) in the background.

In short order, veer right and head steeply up on a well-defined single track. The path crests and drops into a little meadow, where it's lined with stones. The going gets muddy—and sometimes buggy—as you go over blowdowns and brooks. Gently rise among blooms of arctic lupine, corn lily, leatherleaf saxifrage, mountain arnica, partridge-foot, pink monkey-flower, subalpine daisy, and white mountain-heather. Encourage kids to stay on the main path to avoid trampling the slow-growing subalpine vegetation.

Level out in a broad meadow with Heapus Peak looming ahead. Hop a clear stream at the halfway point. Ascend in open terrain. Skirt the base of a boulder field—hoary marmot habitat—beneath a cliff displaying columnar jointing. The cliff and boulders are remnants of the ice-impounded Tricouni Southwest lava flow, composed of basaltic andesite and deposited 10,000 to 12,000 years ago during the late Fraser Glaciation. It's part of the Mount Cayley Volcanic Field.

Keep right and drop down to follow a brook up. Cross the boulder field higher up, with the aid of cairns. Look back to see Cloudburst Mountain (Sáwpa) perfectly framed by the rocky terrain. Ascend the meadow path, passing a pond to your right, to hit the day's high point.

Bypass the outlet and follow intermittent paths right to a promontory overlooking the foot of Berg Lake (49°59′56″ N, 123°14′07″ W). It's a glorious scene. Tricouni Peak commands the head of the windy cirque, where a waterfall feeds the chilly turquoise lake. Boulder slopes and snow patches surround the tarn. Alpine lady ferns huddle on the rocky ground.

Retrace your steps for 1.9 km (1.2 mi) to return to your vehicle. Savour views of Cloudburst Mountain and the Tantalus Range (Tsewílx) during the descent. Pack it in, pack it out. It's vital to put Leave No Trace principles into practice here.

15 Cal-Cheak Trail

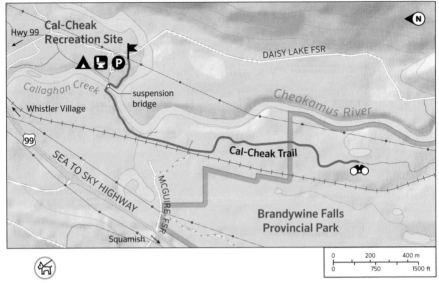

Distance: 3.2 km (2 mi)	**Difficulty:** ■
Elevation gain: 45 m (150 ft)	**Quality:** 😊 😊
High point: 530 m (1,740 ft)	**Map:** Green Trails 92J1S Whistler
Season: spring to fall	**Trailhead:** 50°03′32″ N, 123°06′00″ W

ANY TRAIL with a suspension bridge is solid gold as far as most kids are concerned, right? Well, this one gets off to a fabulous start then. From the Cal-Cheak Recreation Site in Whistler, head to a lake in Brandywine Falls Provincial Park. Enjoy the lovely forest, the volcanic terrain, and maybe even a little trainspotting.

GETTING THERE

Vehicle: Heading north on Highway 99 (Sea to Sky Highway), 45 km (28 mi) north of Downtown Squamish and 13 km (8.1 mi) south of Whistler Village, turn east on Daisy Lake Forest Service Road. (Southbound on Highway 99, go past the turnoff and turn around at Brandywine Falls Provincial Park.) Take the gravel road (2WD) past the

Cal-Cheak Recreation Site's Callaghan Camp and park near the entrance of the south campground (toilet available), by the electricity pylon.

THE HIKE

From the electricity pylon, head west through the south campground, passing an outhouse and campsites 23 and 22. Follow the trail up the stairs and by campsites 21 and 20. Arrive at the suspension bridge over Callaghan Creek (Scwálem to the Líl̓wat Nation, Sts'ák̓'ay̓s to the Squamish Nation), just upstream from its confluence with the Cheakamus River (Nsqwítsu to the Líl̓wat, Ch'iyák̲mesh Stak̲w to the Squamish).

Cross to the right bank and head downstream under tall firs on the virtually unmarked Cal-Cheak Trail. Take a wooden bridge over a creek. At McGuire, the former site of a Pacific Great Eastern Railway station, don't cross the tracks. Go straight across the road to find the trail—which henceforth remains between the Cheakamus River and the Canadian National Railway corridor—in the trees ahead.

After crossing a creek on a plank bridge, bear left, then right, to stay on the path. Ascend between volcanic outcrops and go through an open area with pines. Descend into the forest and pass by ponds. Tread on boardwalk and an old rocky road. Encounter a Brandywine Falls

The suspension bridge over Callaghan Creek (Sts'ák'ay̓s) in winter.

Provincial Park boundary marker, and continue south, negotiating mud and deadfall. Step across a creek. Spot small lakes to the left of the trail. Finally, arrive at the destination lake. Bear left for a rocky viewpoint amid the pines on its west shore (50°02′52″ N, 123°06′26″ W), 1.6 km (1 mi) from the parking area. Behind the pretty swimming hole is a B.C. Hydro power line and, hidden from view, the Cheakamus River. The Black Tusk (Q'elqámtensa ti Skenknápa to the Líĺwat, T'ekt'akmúy̓in tl'a In7iny̓áxa7en to the Squamish), a boundary marker for the territory of the St'át'imc people, provides a magnificent backdrop. Retrace your steps to the Cal-Cheak Recreation Site.

The Cal-Cheak Trail continues south to meet the Sea to Sky Trail (Kaxwísxala to the Líĺwat, An esxwéxwkw shewálh to the Squamish), between the Whistler Bungee Bridge and Brandywine Falls (Cwéscwest to the Líĺwat, Stséxwem to the Squamish). It can be combined with the Lava Lake Trail to form a more challenging loop.

Dogs must be leashed in Brandywine Falls Provincial Park. No drones, fires, flower or mushroom picking, motorized vehicles, smoking, or vaping.

···························· **Fun Fact** ························

When you visit Brandywine Falls Provincial Park, you are walking on lava from a volcano that erupted 13,000 years ago during the Fraser Glaciation. The six-sided black columns you see in the park are made of basalt, and they got their shape when the hot melted rock cooled quickly.

16 Train Wreck Falls

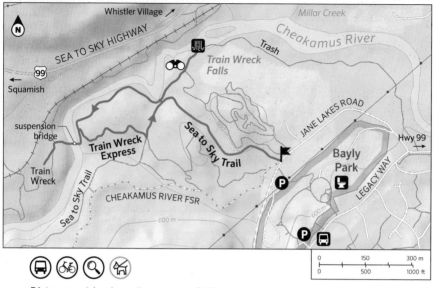

Distance: 2.8 km (1.7 mi)
Elevation gain: 50 m (165 ft)
High point: 610 m (2,000 ft)
Season: spring to fall

Difficulty: ■
Quality: ☺ ☺ ☺
Map: NTS 92-J/3 Brandywine Falls
Trailhead: 50°04′51″ N, 123°02′43″ W

ONCE A LOCALS' HAUNT, Whistler's Train Wreck site is now an essential stop on many a sightseer's itinerary—not to mention a guaranteed kid-pleaser. A suspension bridge over the Cheakamus River (Nsqwítsu to the Lílwat Nation, Ch'iyákmesh Stakw to the Squamish Nation) leads to seven derailed boxcars—covered with garish graffiti and daring mountain-bike jumps—rusting in the woods. Our recommended circuit breaks away from the tourist trail for waterfall views and the possibility of solitude.

GETTING THERE

Transit: Take Whistler Transit Bus 10 (Valley Express) or 20 (Cheakamus) from Whistler Village to Cheakamus Crossing at Bayly Park. Walk

Crossing the Train Wreck Bridge.

west through the park, passing washrooms and a playground and joining the Sea to Sky Trail, to reach the trailhead. (Epic Rides and YVR Skylynx offer daily coach service to Whistler's Gateway Loop from Burrard Station in Vancouver.)

Vehicle: Heading northbound on Highway 99 (Sea to Sky Highway), turn right (south) on Cheakamus Lake Road at Cheakamus Crossing, 7.5 km (4.7 mi) south of Whistler Village. Continue onto Legacy Way and take the bridge over the Cheakamus River. Turn right on Jane Lakes Road. Just past the Cheakamus River Forest Service Road entrance on the right, pull into the parking lot for Bayly Park (1015 Jane Lakes Road; toilet available) on the left.

THE HIKE

Find the Train Wreck trailhead to the right of the Cheakamus River FSR entrance. Pause to read the interpretive panel from the Get Bear Smart Society. Set off west on the Sea to Sky Trail (Kaxwísxala to the Lílwat Nation, An esxwéxwkw shewálh to the Squamish Nation), part of the Trans Canada Trail system. Hardhack, red elderberry, and thimbleberry flower along the wide gravel path through the mixed forest.

In 500 m (0.3 mi), exit the Sea to Sky Trail to the right at an unsigned fork. Keep right to head upstream on the undulating Trash trail. Watch out for mountain bikers. Optional side paths offer precarious vantages of the Cheakamus River's rapids. Keep left at Just Another Bike Trail; before and after this junction, leftward paths lead to excellent viewpoints of the gorge below Train Wreck Falls.

Trash crosses an outcrop beside the waterfall (50°05′02″ N, 123°02′56″ W), 800 m (0.5 mi) from the trailhead. Keep kids off the slippery rock and out of the glacier-fed whitewater. Spot rainbows in the mist. Turn around and head downstream, sticking with Trash for 700 m (0.4 mi) and enjoying the dappled light illuminating the mossy forest floor. Stay on the main track, forking right a few times, to arrive at the east end of the bouncy Train Wreck Bridge (50°04′53″ N, 123°03′16″ W), which opened in 2016.

From a bench and historical panel, cross to river right, holding on to small children by hand. Explore the once-mysterious boxcars scattered among the cedars and firs between the Canadian National Railway line and Cheakamus River. According to the Whistler Museum, the Pacific Great Eastern Railway (the predecessor of B.C. Rail) dumped the cars at this site after a 1956 crash on the route to Parkhurst (Hike 18).

On the way back to the trailhead, take the wide gravel path for a quick exit. Follow Train Wreck Express to the Sea to Sky Trail, turn left, and return to Jane Lakes Road, 1 km (0.6 mi) from the suspension bridge.

Horses and motorized vehicles are prohibited on these trails. Dogs must be leashed.

··················· **Fun Fact** ·····················

Did you know that the Canadian National Railway and Canadian Pacific Railway hire their own private police forces in Canada and the U.S.? Constables with the CN Police Service and CP Police Service are responsible for keeping railway property and everything within 500 m (0.3 mi) of it safe. They have the same powers of arrest as other police officers in Canada.

17 | One Duck Lake | Trail map on p. 90

Distance: 3.2 km (2 mi)
Elevation gain: 90 m (295 ft)
High point: 775 m (2,540 ft)
Season: spring to fall

Difficulty: ◆
Quality: ☺ ☺
Map: Green Trails 92J1S Whistler
Trailhead: 50°09'46" N, 122°55'53" W

ONE DUCK LAKE is a little gem nestled in the No Flow Zone mountain-bike network above Whistler's Emerald Estates. On a hot day, a dip in this swimming hole is ample reward for the short hike. Kids will also enjoy seeking out the Wiffle golf course hidden in these woods.

GETTING THERE

Transit: Take Whistler Transit Bus 10 (Valley Express), 30, or 32 (Emerald) from Whistler Village to Emerald Drive at Pinetree Lane. (Epic Rides and YVR Skylynx offer daily coach service to Whistler's Gateway Loop from Burrard Station in Vancouver.)

Vehicle: On Highway 99 (Sea to Sky Highway), 7.5 km (4.7 mi) north of Whistler Village, turn west on Emerald Drive (one block north of the Emerald Estates sign on Autumn Drive). Go left to stay on Emerald Drive, right on Pinetree Lane, and right on Emerald. Find street parking by the Deerhorn Place intersection.

THE HIKE

From the intersection of Emerald Drive and Deerhorn Place, head northwest on the unsigned Death Chute trail, which starts at the tow-away zone left of the No Campfires Allowed sign and fire hydrant. With tree-anchored handlines for aid, tackle the very steep and loose incline that constitutes the early crux of the hike.

Above the fixed ropes, detour left on a side path. Clamber over deadfall and up rock to a swell viewpoint where a plank resting on boulders serves as a bench. To the east, Mount Cook, Mount Weart, Rethel

A *Wiffle golf course* hidden in the woods.

Mountain, Parkhurst Mountain, and Wedge Mountain tower behind the glacial milk of Green Lake, at the headwaters of the Green River (Emhátkwa in Ucwalmícwts, the language of the Líĺwat Nation). Continue up Death Chute, which immediately levels out, paralleling Rideau Brook.

Meet a gravel road and go left. Ignore side paths for 200 m (220 yd). Where a big Campfires Are Not Permitted sign is nailed to a tree, make a hard turn onto the road that joins from the right (or use the shortcut path immediately before this junction).

Just up the gentle road, which is part of the Shit Happens bike trail, investigate clearings in the trees to the right. Find a tee and hole belonging to a Wiffle golf course. This variation of golf uses the perforated plastic ball of childhood memories.

Keep left at a messy junction with the Azrael bike path to stay on the main trail, though a narrow path parallels it on the right; the tracks merge on an outcrop. Pass the entrance to Trial and Error on the left. At a green No Fires and No Camping sign (get the hint?), turn right off Shit Happens and descend to the shore of One Duck Lake (50°09′52″ N, 122°56′41″ W). Go forth to the gravel neck dividing the lake from a neighbouring pond, after 1.7 km (1.1 mi) on foot.

Hardhack blooms with pink flowers at the welcoming lake, which sits in a bowl at the base of a boulder slope. From the neck, the path continues uphill to a sketchy rope swing and tree ladder by a cairn. After a stop to eat, drink, and rest—and perhaps swim—head back down the way you came.

One Duck Lake lies in the territories of the Líĺwat and Squamish First Nations. Stay alert and step aside to allow mountain bikers to pass.

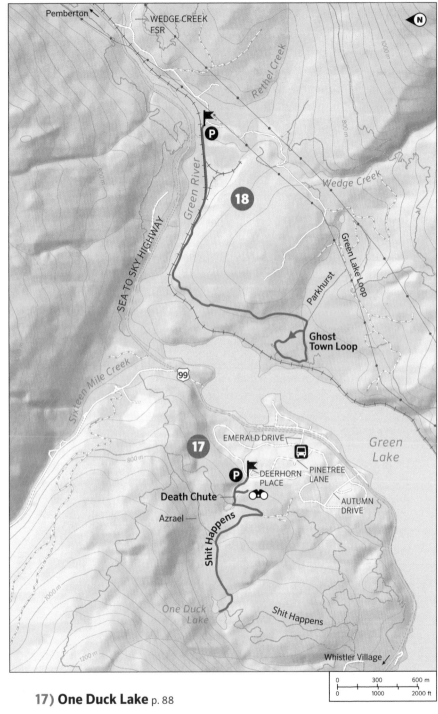

17) One Duck Lake p. 88

18) Parkhurst Ghost Town p. 91

18 Parkhurst Ghost Town | Photo on p. 18

Distance: 5.6 km (3.5 mi)
Elevation gain: 80 m (260 ft)
High point: 700 m (2,300 ft)
Season: spring to fall

Difficulty: ■
Quality: ☺ ☺
Map: NTS 92-J/2 Whistler
Trailhead: 50°09′56″ N, 122°53′46″ W

IN HORROR FILMS such as *Silent Hill*, *House of Wax*, and *The Hills Have Eyes*, ghost towns are damned places people should avoid at all costs. Pay a daytime visit to Whistler's ghost town and give the kids a few stories to tell. It's peaceful amid the cabin ruins and vehicle hulks of Parkhurst.

GETTING THERE

Vehicle: On Highway 99 (Sea to Sky Highway), 12 km (7.5 mi) north of Whistler Village, turn east on Wedge Creek Forest Service Road (signed for Garibaldi Provincial Park's Wedgemount Lake). Cross the Canadian National Railway track and bear right to go over the Green River bridge. Keep right at two junctions on the gravel road (2WD). Park in a pullout on the right, 1 km (0.6 mi) from the highway, where there's a concrete blockade at road's end and a yellow gate on the spur to the left.

THE HIKE

On foot, continue west on the gravel road beyond the graffitied blockade. Carefully cross Wedge Creek on a sketchy bridge, upstream from a Canadian National Railway span and the glacial-floured creek's confluence with the Green River (Emhátkwa in Ucwalmícwts, the language of the Lílwat Nation). On the other side, there's a picnic table and then an unsigned trail entrance to the left. Spurning the Green Lake Loop, forge ahead on the road.

Enter the railway corridor, where one track splits into three. When it's safe to do so, cross the leftmost track. Look back to admire Mount Cook, Mount Weart, and Rethel Mountain rising to the east in Garibaldi Provincial Park. Follow the boot path through the rocks to the left of the other two tracks until three tracks become one again. A Green Lake Loop/Parkhurst sign directs you back into the shady trees on the left, where you join an old road.

Ignore a steep path on the left. Where the road heads down and to the right, fork left onto a hiking and snowshoeing trail occasionally marked with orange flagging tape. Soon a marsh is visible through the trees to the right. Ascend, with steep bits and minor deadfall, to a blufftop where trees obscure the view of Green Lake. Continue southward over gentle ups and downs. Bunchberry and red and black huckleberry bear fruit under the conifers.

At a signpost, 2.3 km (1.4 mi) from your start, turn right for the Ghost Town Loop (50°09′31″ N, 122°54′57″ W). (To the left, the Parkhurst Trail crosses a creek on a bridge.) Fork right to go counterclockwise.

Parkhurst was once the site of the first large sawmill in Whistler, previously named Alta Lake and initially Summit Lake. Located on the Pacific Great Eastern Railway line and the shore of Green Lake, the original Parkhurst Mill started up in 1920s and burned down in the '30s. The rebuilt sawmill operated until the '50s, after which the associated settlement went into decline.

Stroll the wide path, encountering a smashed-up car, ramshackle cabin and outhouse, and rusted-out truck—all covered in colourful graffiti. The remains of cabins no longer standing, bed frames, appliances, and bottles are strewn about the woods. Keep left on the main path, finish the 900-m (0.6-mi) loop, turn left at the Parkhurst–Ghost Town Loop junction, and retrace your steps to the parking area.

The Resort Municipality of Whistler bought the Parkhurst site, which lies in the territories of the Líl̓wat and Squamish First Nations, in 2017. No camping, fires, fireworks, flower picking, horses, or motorized vehicles. Dogs must be leashed. To learn about local history, visit the Whistler Museum (4333 Main Street), adjacent to Florence Petersen Park, in Whistler Village.

19 Ancient Cedars Trail

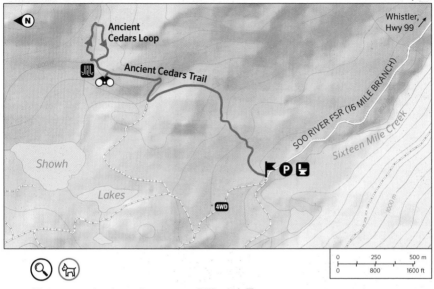

Distance: 4.7 km (2.9 mi)
Elevation gain: 189 m (620 ft)
High point: 1,030 m (3,380 ft)
Season: late spring to early fall

Difficulty: ■
Quality: ☺ ☺
Map: Green Trails 92J1s Whistler
Trailhead: 50°11'40" N, 122°57'35" W

AROUND 700 YEARS AGO, Marco Polo travelled the Silk Road to China and a pandemic known as the Black Death killed millions of people in Eurasia and Africa. Meanwhile, on the other side of the world, seedlings of western red cedar and yellow-cedar took root on Cougar Mountain, north of Whistler. Take a hike on the family-friendly Ancient Cedars Trail, in the territories of the Líl̓wat and Squamish First Nations, to commune with these centuries-old giants.

GETTING THERE

Vehicle: On Highway 99 (Sea to Sky Highway), 8.7 km (5.4 mi) north of Whistler Village, turn west on Soo River Forest Service Road (16 Mile Branch), also known as Cougar Mountain Road. The Ancient Cedars

Old-growth western red cedars on Cougar Mountain.

A waterfall at the Ancient Cedars Loop.

trailhead (toilet available) is 4.3 km (2.7 mi) up the rough gravel road (possible with high-clearance 2WD, but 4WD recommended). Park on the left at the Showh Lakes fork.

THE HIKE

From the trailhead kiosk, head northeast on a smooth gravel path into the woods. Wooden box culverts divert water off the well-built Ancient Cedars Trail, which is marked with reflective orange diamonds. Bunchberry and Sitka columbine bloom on the forest floor. Pass a glacial erratic.

Bear left at a rock wall with boulders at its base. Zigzag steadily upward, now with roots and rocks on the wide trail bed. The grade eases and then the path descends. A marsh lies at the bottom of a boulder slope to the right; a bench on the left invites a rest or snack stop.

At a signposted junction, meet a rough 4×4 road from Showh Lakes and turn right. Fork right off the loose road to go up several steps at a leftward bend; quickly rejoin the road. Pass a memorial log bench. Detour left for a signed viewpoint. From the lovely bluff, look out at Showh Lakes, surrounded by trees, and up the Soo River (Sú7a in Ucwalmícwts, the language of the Líl̓wat Nation) valley to Numbers Peak.

Cross a creek on a wooden bridge to start the clockwise Ancient Cedars Loop (50°12′16″ N, 122°56′58″ W), after 2 km (1.2 mi) on foot. Pass a wetland with skunk cabbage. Take in the sight of a segmented waterfall off to the left. Benches and interpretive panels invite you to pause and contemplate the massive western red cedars, surrounded by devil's club, in the quiet old-growth grove. Kids can investigate the trees' big burls and little hollows. Thanks to campaigning by the Western Canada Wilderness Committee in the 1980s, these giants were spared the logger's axe.

Go over a bridge and finish the 700 m (0.4 mi) loop. Turn left and retrace your steps to Soo River FSR.

The Ancient Cedars Trail is located on provincial land in Cheakamus Community Forest, which is co-managed by the Líl̓wat Nation, Squamish Nation, and Resort Municipality of Whistler. No fireworks, littering, motorized vehicles, shooting, or tree cutting. Dogs must be under control at all times.

·················· **Fun Fact** ··················

Sḵwiḵw, the Sḵwx̱wú7mesh name for Whistler, is the word for "marmot" in the language of the Squamish Nation. If you visit the resort municipality—and its nearby mountain—you'll understand how Whistler got its name. Listen for the call of the hoary marmot, which lives in burrows on the slopes of the mountain and above the treeline.

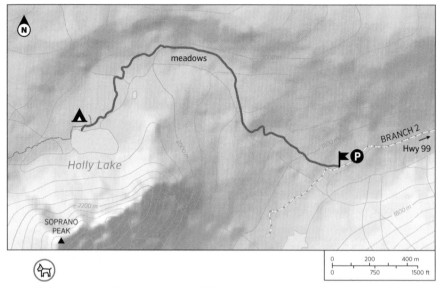

Distance: 4.3 km (2.7 mi)
Elevation gain: 245 m (800 ft)
High point: 2,015 m (6,610 ft)
Season: summer

Difficulty: ◆
Quality: ☺ ☺ ☺
Map: NTS 92-J/9 Shalalth
Trailhead: 50°34′35″ N, 122°15′58″ W

WATCH BEES and butterflies pollinate meadows of riotous wildflowers. Take a dip in a chilly mountain lake, if you dare. Stare up at rocky peaks and contemplate future scrambles. A hike in the splendid Downton Creek basin will give youngsters a taste of the subalpine they won't soon forget.

GETTING THERE

Vehicle: From Whistler, head north on Highway 99 (Sea to Sky Highway). In Mount Currie, turn right to stay on Highway 99 (Duffey Lake Road) for 68 km (42 mi). Just past the Cottonwood Recreation Site (toilet available), turn left on Downton Creek Forest Service Road. (From Hope, take Trans-Canada Highway 1 eastbound. In Lytton, turn left on Highway 12 [Main Street/KEEya] and left again to stay on Highway 12

Holly Lake behind Lorna Lake and Soprano Peak.

[Lytton-Lillooet Highway]. In Lillooet, turn left on Highway 99 [Duffey Lake Road] and drive 24 km [15 mi]. Turn right on Downton Creek FSR.) Immediately, cross the Cayoosh Creek bridge and ignore two left-hand spurs. Pass a gated quarry on your right. Cross Downton Creek five times before the 5-km (3.1-mi) marker, then stay right at a fork. After 10.5 km (6.5 mi) on the mainline, turn right on signed Branch 2 (2WD with decent clearance). Drive up the narrow gravel road—through the encroaching vegetation and wide, shallow water bars—and park at a landing, 14 km (8.7 mi) from the highway.

THE HIKE

Spot cairns on both sides of the logging road at the far end of the landing (1,770 m/5,810 ft). Soprano Peak looms large ahead. The trailhead is on the right, indicated by a wooden arrow and pink flagging. Set off west in the regenerating clear-cut—brightened by arctic lupine, fireweed, Sitka valerian, and subalpine daisy—and into the forest. Zigzag uphill on the narrow path, which is steep and muddy at times. After pulling alongside a creek to your left, the grade slackens.

After 700 m (0.4 mi), enter the first of the subalpine meadows, adding edible thistle, fringed grass-of-Parnassus, pink wintergreen, and scarlet paintbrush to the floral mix. Spy blue butterflies and longhorn beetles on the blossoms, and quartz embedded in the ground. Pass a snag varnished by its own sap.

Re-enter the trees, including subalpine firs and whitebark pines, 1.3 km (0.8 mi) from the trailhead, and go up a bit. Step over a brook, encounter an old B.C. Forest Service hiking trail marker affixed to a trunk, and catch your breath at the high point by a big boulder. Descend and pass little ponds as the trees give way to muddy meadows. Cross a clear creek, 1.8 km (1.1 mi) in, and then a muddy brook amid the heather, with the air scented like Cindy Cinnamon from the Jelly Bean Dolls of the 1980s.

Head upstream on the left bank of a creek to the outlet of alluring Holly Lake, by a sizable boulder and the first tent sites. Continue right on the main lakeshore path, passing social trails and rock fire rings (please don't build fires in the subalpine!), to reach a little promontory with boulders and a wide-angle view of the lake (2,000 m/6,560 ft; 50°34′41″ N, 122°17′08″ W), after 2.1 km (1.3 mi) on foot.

Soprano Peak fills the scene, standing tall with intrusive rock pillars, a cave on its north face, and a talus apron, across the Tiffany blue water. Listen for the whistles of marmots and pikas and the calls of grouse and ptarmigan. Watch the fish jumping—or join them in the lake. To the west, Contralto Peak, Schroeder Peak, Linus Mountain, and Faulty Tower oversee the head of the Holly Lake basin. Retrace your steps to the trailhead.

The Downton Creek drainage lies in the territory of the St'át'imc people. Downton is a tributary of Cayoosh Creek (Nlháxten in Ucwalmícwts, the language of the Líỻwat Nation). Be prepared for unexpected weather changes. Please stick to established trails and tent sites to preserve the slow-growing subalpine vegetation. Leave No Trace practices are imperative in this environment. Motorized vehicles are prohibited at elevations higher than 1,920 m (6,300 ft) in the Cayoosh Range.

·················· **Fun Fact** ··················

Can you spot the theme for unofficially named Contralto Peak and Soprano Peak, along with nearby Mezzo Peak and Tenor Peak? In classical music, a soprano has the highest vocal range among female singers, a contralto has the lowest range, and a mezzo-soprano's range lies in between. Among male singers, a tenor has the second-highest vocal range—lower than a countertenor and higher than both a baritone and a bass.

21 Burnaby Mountain (Lhu<u>k</u>w'lhu<u>k</u>w'áyten)

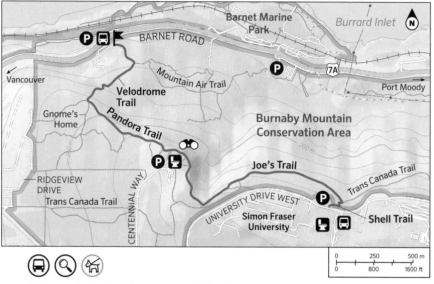

Distance: 6.5 km (4 mi)
Elevation gain: 290 m (950 ft)
High point: 330 m (1,080 ft)
Season: all year

Difficulty: ◆
Quality: ☺
Map: NTS 92-G/7 Port Coquitlam
Trailhead: 49°17′22″ N, 122°56′24″ W

KNOWN AS Lhu<u>k</u>w'lhu<u>k</u>w'áyten ("where the bark gets peeled in spring") in S<u>k</u>w<u>x</u>wú7mesh sníchim, the language of the Squamish Nation, Burnaby Mountain (370 m/1,210 ft) is the highest point on the Burrard Peninsula at the core of Metro Vancouver. The steep Velodrome Trail is a heart-pounding way to reach the sandstone and conglomerate cuesta's summit plateau, occupied by Simon Fraser University. Family-friendly attractions include a playground and large picnic area. Taking public transit makes possible a one-way hike, in either direction, which cuts the distance in half.

Transit: Take TransLink Bus 160 (Kootenay Loop/Port Coquitlam Station) to the 7500 block of Barnet Road.

Vehicle: From Vancouver, head east on Hastings Street (formerly Highway 7A). In Burnaby, continue onto Inlet Drive, which becomes Barnet Road. (Alternatively, from Highway 7 [Lougheed Highway] in Coquitlam, head west on Barnet Highway [formerly Highway 7A]. Continue onto St. Johns Street in Port Moody. Go right on Barnet Highway, which becomes Barnet Road in Burnaby.) At the Kask Bros./Velodrome intersection, 1.2 km (0.7 mi) west of Barnet Marine Park, turn north and pull into the Velodrome Trail's gravel parking lot.

THE HIKE

Burnaby's answer to the Grouse Grind, the Velodrome Trail climbs more than 500 stairs on its way up the north-facing escarpment of Burnaby Mountain, which is officially named Mount Burnaby. Find the trailhead at the northeast corner of the Harry Jerome Sports Centre (7564 Barnet Road), which houses an indoor velodrome (bicycle-racing track), across the street and up the driveway (250 m/270 yd) from the trail parking lot.

Set off on the wide gravel path of the dual-use Mountain Air Trail. Go right at the first junction in the shady mixed woods to start up the hiking-only Velodrome Trail. (The Mountain Air Trail continues east to the Mountain Air Bike Skills Park and Barnet Marine Park, both alternative parking spots for this hike.)

Tackle the stairs (try counting them!), with the help of rope railings, and zigzag up the mountainside. Take a breather on a bench halfway up the steps. Enjoy the greenery, including deer, licorice, and spiny wood ferns. At the top of the stairs, 800 m (0.5 mi) from the trailhead, turn left on the Pandora Trail.

Immediately, keep left at Gnome's Home. Follow the steepening dirt path along the fence guarding the cliffs to the left and lined with Oregon grape and salal. Pass through a gate and emerge in a big field. Follow the path, gravel then paved, through the sublime *Kamui Mintara (Playground of the Gods)* sculptures, wood-carved by Ainu artists Nuburi Toko and Shusei Toko to commemorate the sister-city relationship of Burnaby and Kushiro, Japan.

The top of the Velodrome Trail.

Descending the stairs of the Velodrome Trail.

Pull back alongside the fence and continue uphill. Stop to read an interpretive panel about the geology of the Coast Mountains, Burnaby Mountain, and nearby Capitol Hill. Reach a stone monument indicating the cardinal directions (280 m/920 ft), 900 m (0.6 mi) from the top of the Velodrome Trail. From the clifftop viewpoint, gaze north at Mount Seymour, Burrard Inlet and Indian Arm (Tsleil-Wat in hǝṅ̓q̓ǝmiṅ̓ǝm̓, the language of the Tsleil-Waututh Nation), and Belcarra Mountain, with Meslilloet Mountain beckoning in the distance.

Closer at hand are the Burnaby Centennial Rose Garden, the Centennial Pavilion washrooms, a playground, and countless picnic tables and benches. The parking lot, a make-out point featured in the 2003 film *My Life Without Me*, affords outstanding views of Vancouver at sunset. Continue upward on the Pandora Trail, following the fence and keeping left to merge with the Trans Canada Trail (TCT, officially rebranded as the Great Trail) at a level section. Pass a water tower painted with orcas and sea jellies.

Go left at a kiosk to stick with the TCT. Bigleaf maple, red alder, and western red cedar trees flourish along Joe's Trail, which provided my first-year biology class at SFU with plenty of examples of nurse logs and forest succession. ("It's so quiet here," my eight-year-old son observed, before we heard a train horn from the Canadian Pacific Railway tracks below.)

At a three-way junction with a kiosk, turn right, leaving the TCT. Head steeply up Shell Trail to pop out of the woods on University Drive West (49°16'49" N, 122°55'16" W) by the SFU Transportation Centre, 3.3 km (2.1 mi) from the trailhead. Retrace your steps to the velodrome to complete an out-and-back trip. Uphill-only hikers can catch TransLink Bus R5 (Hastings Street), 144 (Metrotown Station), or 145 (Production Station) off the mountain. Transit makes the other one-way option—from top to bottom—a less-sweaty possibility too.

The Burnaby Mountain Conservation Area lies in the territories of the Musqueam, Qayqayt, Squamish, and Tsleil-Waututh First Nations. Trails are open dawn to dusk. Potential wildlife sightings include coast moles, Columbian black-tailed deer, coyotes, raccoons, ravens, and, only rarely, black bears. Dogs must be leashed.

22 Jug Island Beach | Trail map on p. 106

Distance: 5.2 km (3.2 mi)
Elevation gain: 85 m (280 ft)
High point: 85 m (280 ft)
Season: all year

Difficulty: ■
Quality: ☺ ☺
Map: Canadian Map Makers Coquitlam; Trail Ventures PoMo
Trailhead: 49°18′46″ N, 122°55′30″ W

WHETHER YOU hike from Belcarra or kayak from Deep Cove (Guyangulton in hən̓q̓əmi̓nəm̓, the language of the Tsleil-Waututh Nation), Jug Island Beach in Belcarra Regional Park is an enchanting destination. The concave shoreline hosts barnacles, crabs, limpets, sea stars, and dramatically fractured, multicoloured rock. Search the treetops and sky for bald eagles.

GETTING THERE

Transit: Take TransLink Bus 182 (Belcarra) from Moody Centre Station to Bedwell Bay Road at Midden Road.

Vehicle: From Barnet Highway (formerly Highway 7A) in Port Moody, 2.2 km (1.4 mi) west of Highway 7 (Lougheed Highway), go north on Ioco Road. In two blocks, turn left to stay on Ioco for another 4 km (2.5 mi). Make a right on First Avenue, then keep left for Bedwell Bay Road. In 1.7 km (1.1 mi), turn left at a three-way stop. Enter the Belcarra Regional Park gates. (Note the posted closing time.) Take Tumtumay-whueton Drive to the Belcarra Picnic Area parking lot (toilet available) at road's end. Make sure to slow down at the Newts Crossing sign en route.

THE HIKE

The Belcarra Peninsula is the site of Tum-tumay-whueton, the Tsleil-Waututh Nation's largest ancestral winter village. The grassy mound at the Belcarra Picnic Area hides a large shell midden and looks out at Kapulpaqua (the hən̓q̓əmi̓nəm̓ name for the entrance to Indian

Jug Island in Indian Arm (Tsleil-Wat).

Looking up Indian Arm (Tsleil-Wat) from Jug Island Beach.

Arm [Tsleil-Wat]). Find the trailhead next to the picnic shelters and playground—hopefully you make it farther than this point!

Follow the gravel path northeast to Bedwell Bay Road; cross by the bus stop. Pass the Bedwell Bay Trail and turn right to start the well-trafficked Jug Island Beach Trail (no bikes). Quickly fork left at the next signpost. The roadbed rises in the second-growth forest, bears right where a log fence is ahead, and levels out.

Fork right at a signpost to leave the roadbed, after 1.6 km (1 mi) on foot. Pass under a rock wall covered with weeping moss, go up wooden stairs, and scamper over a few little outcrops. Under a power line, a partial viewpoint overlooks Bedwell Bay. Descend the muddy path, with the aid of stone steps, noticing rusted artifacts on the forest floor and passing an outhouse. Emerge from the forest at Jug Island Beach (49°19′47″ N, 122°54′56″ W), 2.6 km (1.6 mi) from the Belcarra Picnic Area.

Comb the beach for interesting rocks and shells but remember the fourth principle of Leave No Trace: "Leave what you find." Look at and listen to the waves. Gaze up the fjord of Indian Arm at Mount Bonnycastle, Little Horn Mountain, and Racoon Island. Racoon is part of Say Nuth Khaw Yum Provincial Park, which is co-managed by the Tsleil-Waututh and B.C. Parks. (It's also where, at six years old, I slept under a tarp for the first time during a week at the YMCA of Greater Vancouver's Camp Howdy, established in 1947.) Retrace your steps to the trailhead.

Belcarra Regional Park lies in the territories of the Musqueam, Qayqayt, Squamish, and Tsleil-Waututh First Nations. No balloons, camping, feeding wildlife, fires, fireworks, foraging, guns, littering, or smoking or vaping (except in designated areas). Dogs must be leashed.

························· **Fun Fact** ·······················

The name of Say Nuth Khaw Yum Provincial Park—originally called Indian Arm Provincial Park in 1995—means "Serpent's Land" in hən̓q̓əmin̓əm̓, the language of the Tsleil-Waututh Nation. It honours stories passed down over generations about a two-headed serpent in Indian Arm (Tsleil-Wat).

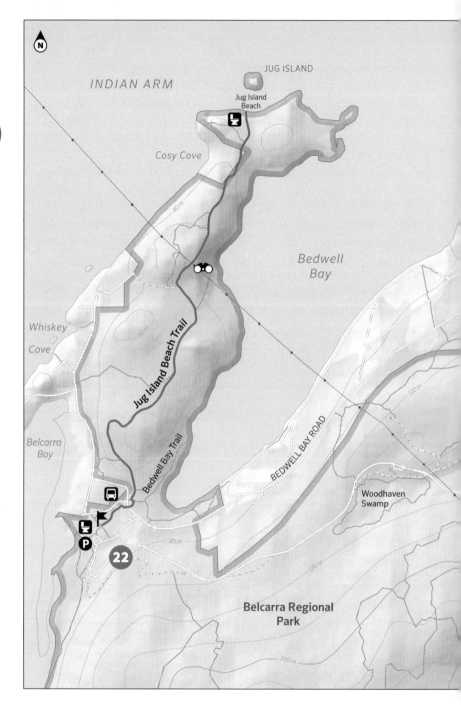

INDIAN ARM

JUG ISLAND

Jug Island Beach

Cosy Cove

Bedwell Bay

Whiskey Cove

Jug Island Beach Trail

Belcarra Bay

Bedwell Bay Trail

BEDWELL BAY ROAD

Woodhaven Swamp

22

Belcarra Regional Park

22) Jug Island Beach p. 103 / **23) Sasamat Lake** p. 108

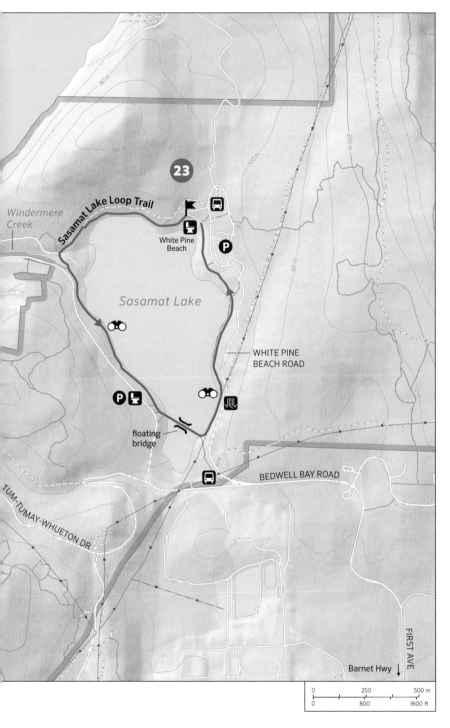

23

Windermere
Creek

Sasamat Lake Loop Trail

White Pine
Beach

Sasamat Lake

WHITE PINE
BEACH ROAD

floating
bridge

TUM-TUMAY-WHUETON DR

BEDWELL BAY ROAD

FIRST AVE

Barnet Hwy

0	250	500 m
0	800	1600 ft

23 Sasamat Lake | Trail map on p. 107; photo on p. 234

Distance: 3.2 km (2 mi)
Elevation gain: 20 m (65 ft)
High point: 60 m (200 ft)
Season: all year

Difficulty: ●
Quality: ☺ ☺
Map: Canadian Map Makers Coquitlam;
Trail Ventures PoMo
Trailhead: 49°19′30″ N, 122°53′16″ W

LOOKING FOR a no-fail place to introduce young kids to the joys of getting out in nature? No matter the season or weather, get thee to Sasamat Lake in Belcarra Regional Park. Little ones will find trees to hug, bridges to cross, a waterfall to visit, and a lake to splash in.

GETTING THERE

Transit: From Coquitlam Central Station, take TransLink Bus 150 (White Pine Beach) to its terminus. This seasonal service runs on weekends and holidays from May to September and weekdays from July to September. Alternatively, Bus 182 (Belcarra) offers year-round service from Moody Centre Station to Bedwell Bay Road at White Pine Beach Road. Behind the park gate, take the path on the left to join the Sasamat Lake Loop Trail by the floating bridge.

Vehicle: From Barnet Highway (formerly Highway 7A) in Port Moody, 2.2 km (1.4 mi) west of Highway 7 (Lougheed Highway), go north on Ioco Road. In two blocks, turn left to stay on Ioco for another 4 km (2.5 mi). Make a right on First Avenue, then keep left for Bedwell Bay Road. In 1.2 km (0.7 mi), use the right lane to enter Belcarra Regional Park's White Pine Beach gate. (Note the posted closing time.) Park in one of the six lots (toilet available).

THE HIKE

Follow signs down to White Pine Beach. (Hikers with dogs must use the signed Beach By-Pass to avoid this pet-free zone.) Find the start of the Sasamat Lake Loop Trail (no bikes) at the north end of the main beach, between the shoreline and the picnic tables. The wide gravel path features 12 bridges and 147 steps. Cross the first little bridge, bear left, go through a gate, and merge with the Beach By-Pass.

Breathe in the fresh scent of Douglas-fir and western red cedar. Ascend steps to a gravel road. Turn left, pass a yellow gate, and cross the driveway of the Association of Neighbourhood Houses of B.C.'s Sasamat Outdoor Centre, after 1 km (0.6 mi) of the pleasant counterclockwise loop. Pick up the trail on the other side. Take a larger bridge over Lower Windermere Creek (also known as Crayfish Creek), the lake's outlet to Indian Arm (Tsleil-Wat in hən̓q̓əmin̓əm̓, the language of the Tsleil-Waututh Nation).

Go left at the next junction, spurning the trail to Woodhaven Swamp. Follow the outdoor education centre's tall wooden fence by a high ropes course. Pass a log bench. Earn a couple of viewpoints, offering a look back at White Pine Beach and the dam at the lake's outlet. An outhouse is off to the right, just before the floating bridge at the lakehead. Cross the "floatwalk" (slippery when icy), which has swimming decks and offers a view of Mount Seymour and Buntzen Ridge (Kwe kwe xau). Look for bats at dusk.

At the floating bridge's east end (49°18′58″ N, 122°53′12″ W), meet the trail from the park gate and turn left, after 2 km (1.2 mi) on foot. Tread on a boardwalk, stop to admire a cascade, and come to another boardwalk with cattails and more views. You might spot bald eagles in the trees. Finally, keep left at the Beach By-Pass, go through a gate, and pass the washrooms to return to the main beach.

Belcarra Regional Park lies in the territories of the Musqueam, Qayqayt, Squamish, and Tsleil-Waututh First Nations. In 2020, the Tsleil-Waututh and Metro Vancouver signed an agreement to work together to protect and enhance the park. No alcohol, balloons, camping, feeding wildlife, fires, fireworks, foraging, guns, littering, or smoking or vaping (except in designated areas). Dogs must be leashed and are not permitted on the swimming decks of the floating bridge. Parking is at a premium on hot summer days.

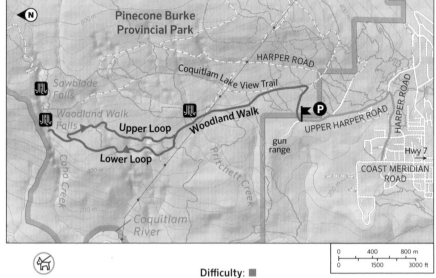

Distance: 9 km (5.6 mi)
Elevation gain: 175 m (575 ft)
High point: 495 m (1,625 ft)
Season: most of the year

Difficulty: ■
Quality: ☺ ☺
Map: Canadian Map Makers Coquitlam;
Trail Ventures PoMo
Trailhead: 49°18′49″ N, 122°44′56″ W

THE WOODLAND WALK traverses the western slopes of Burke Mountain above the Coquitlam River (kwikwetl'em in hənq̓əmiṅəṁ, the language of the Kwikwetlem First Nation). Found in under-the-radar Pinecone Burke Provincial Park and wholly within Coquitlam's city limits, this lollipop hike visits waterfalls and remnants of old-growth forest. It's agreeable on a rainy day as well as in winter, when icicles, hoarfrost, and frozen puddles will delight the young and not-so-young.

GETTING THERE

Vehicle: From Highway 7 (Lougheed Highway) in Port Coquitlam, 2 km (1.2 mi) west of the Pitt River Bridge, go north on Lougheed-Meridian Connector. Turn left on Coast Meridian Road and enter Coquitlam. In

5 km (3.1 mi), turn right on Harper Road. Drive 2 km (1.2 mi) farther—turning left on Upper Harper Road and trading pavement for gravel (2WD)—to find the Pinecone Burke Provincial Park gate on the right, outside of the Port Coquitlam and District Hunting and Fishing Club. Park on the shoulder, but not in the club's driveway.

THE HIKE

From the park gate, kiosk, and boundary marker, head east up the gravel road and away from the noisy outdoor shooting range (closed Tuesdays). Take the first road on the left, which serves as the Coquitlam Lake View Trail. Ignore mountain bike trails on both sides. At a fork in the road, 800 m (0.5 mi) from the gate, go left to start the Woodland Walk. Cross a few creeks, one with a rusted rail lying over it. Pass more bike paths.

Turn left on a road in a big power-line corridor, after 1.8 km (1.1 mi) on foot. Pause on the bridge over Pritchett Creek to admire the cascades immediately upstream and downstream, which are especially dazzling when frozen. Follow the road northeast, passing the signed entrance of the Upper Loop of the Woodland Walk (right) as well as a trail to the Coquitlam River (left).

Continue on the power-line road to find the start of the Lower Loop on the right (49°19'42" N, 122°45'15" W), 500 m (0.3 mi) from the Pritchett Creek bridge. Leave the mountain bikers and sound of gunfire behind. Tread north on the mud and loose rock of the old roadbed, which is marked with blue squares. Rock-hop over a creek. Take the left fork signed for the falls. (Right connects to the Upper Loop.) Cross a couple more creeks.

Keep left at the next junction. The trail goes by a gargantuan western red cedar stump that screams for a grainy photo op. Reach Woodland Walk Falls (49°20'26" N, 122°45'03" W), after 4.5 km (2.8 mi) of hiking. Here a big old-growth Douglas-fir stands over Coho Creek. Carefully descend the steep bank to eye a cascade tumbling over rock and into a clear pool. Keep kids off the slippery rocks and away from the bone-chilling water. Steeper, more dramatic waterfalls are found upstream but trickier to access.

Although a rough path heads uphill by the falls (providing access to a viewpoint and Sawblade Falls), backtrack 500 m (0.3 mi) to the previous junction. Turn left (east) and then right on the gentle Upper Loop. Follow multicoloured markers south through the large stumps (spot a

A frozen cascade on Pritchett Creek.

An old-growth Douglas-fir towers over Coho Creek.

hollow one?); try to imagine the forest pre-logging. Cross streams using a bridge, boulders, and a plank. A little boardwalk eases passage over a wet patch. The Upper Loop bears left to meet the power-line road from earlier. Make a left to revisit the Pritchett Creek cascades and retrace your steps to the park gate.

The Woodland Walk lies in the territories of the Kwikwetlem and Stó:lō First Nations. Pinecone Burke Provincial Park was legislated into existence in 1995, thanks to the efforts of the Burke Mountain Naturalists and other environmentalists. No drones, fires, foraging for fungi or plants, motorized vehicles, smoking, or vaping. Dogs must be leashed. As Coquitlam Search and Rescue advises, if you can see snow on the North Shore peaks, expect snow on Burke Mountain too.

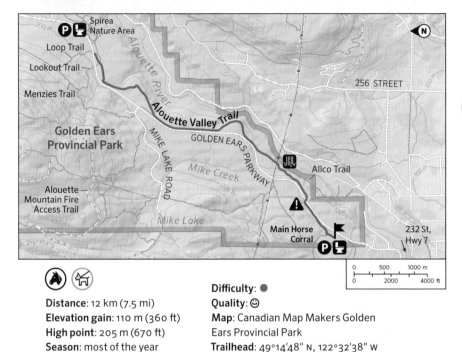

Distance: 12 km (7.5 mi)
Elevation gain: 110 m (360 ft)
High point: 205 m (670 ft)
Season: most of the year

Difficulty: ●
Quality: ☺
Map: Canadian Map Makers Golden Ears Provincial Park
Trailhead: 49°14'48" N, 122°32'38" W

THE ALOUETTE VALLEY TRAIL is an excellent place to introduce kids to the simple joys of forest walking. If they're horse lovers, even better. Equestrians and pedestrians share this wide path in Golden Ears Provincial Park.

GETTING THERE

Vehicle: Heading east on Highway 7 (Lougheed Highway) in Maple Ridge, turn left onto Dewdney Trunk Road, 5 km (3.1 mi) east of the Pitt River Bridge. (On Trans-Canada Highway 1, take Exit 57 in Surrey or Exit 58 in Langley. Follow signs for the Golden Ears Bridge, take the Maple Ridge exit, and continue onto Dewdney Trunk.) In 6 km (3.7 mi), make a left on 232 Street. At the traffic circle, go right on 132 Avenue/

Young hikers on the Alouette Valley Trail.
PHOTO: BRITTANY BRYDON

Fern Crescent. Stay on Fern, bear left onto 128 Avenue, and rejoin Fern, which becomes Golden Ears Parkway. Just past the Golden Ears Provincial Park gate, turn left into the Main Horse Corral parking lot (toilet available). The gate is closed 11 p.m. to 7 a.m. from April to mid-October, and 5:30 p.m. to 8 a.m. from mid-October to March.

THE HIKE
Running from the Main Horse Corral to Alouette Lake's South Beach area, the Alouette Valley Trail mostly stays between Golden Ears Parkway and the Alouette River (sa'anəsaʔł to the Katzie First Nation, Sa'nisalh to the Stó:lō people). Your hike begins at the north corner of the parking lot, between the hitching rack and water pump (for livestock only), and opposite the Mike Lake Trail kiosk. Deer, lady, and sword ferns line the level path.

Quickly turn right at the first junction. (Straight goes to Mike Lake, a family-friendly outing for another day.) Pass the 0.5-km (0.3-mi) marker and pull alongside Golden Ears Parkway. Go up the first little incline and carefully cross the road (watch out for speeding vehicles) to find the 0.88-km (0.5-mi) marker on the other side. Keep your eyes peeled for Pacific banana slugs on the path and vegetation.

After 1.5 km (0.9 mi) on foot, arrive at a junction with the Allco Trail (49°15'15" N, 122°31'46" W), which heads right to a ford on the Alouette River. The Alouette Valley Trail continues straight over Mike Creek on a wooden bridge immediately upstream of a weir. However, detour down Allco and quickly go left to visit a pretty waterfall otherwise hidden from view. (For a short but satisfying outing, turn back here.)

Back on the Alouette Valley Trail, cross a big power-line corridor. Salmonberry and thimbleberry shrubs line the double track as you re-enter the forest. Stay right at a fork after the 2-km (1.2-mi) marker. The path repeatedly sidles up to the parkway—which utilizes an old logging rail bed—then returns to the woods.

Reach a key fork (49°16′24″ N, 122°31′01″ W) at the 4.2-km (2.6-mi) marker. (Left provides access to Mike Lake Road and the south end of the Menzies Trail, across the parkway.) Go right, take a wooden bridge over a stream, and rock-hop another creek below an artificial waterfall spilling forth from a culvert. Ah, don't you love the smell of skunk cabbage in the morning? The path is muddy under the red alder and vine maple trees.

Meet the Lookout Trail at a four-way junction with a map of the Spirea Nature Area. Continue straight forward to find the 6-km (3.7-mi) marker and another Spirea map, beside the parkway (49°16′56″ N, 122°30′11″ W). This is an opportune spot to turn around and retrace your footsteps to the Main Horse Corral.

Alternatively, if your party is up for a lollipop of intermediate difficulty, cross the parkway, ascend the Loop Trail, and go left on the Menzies Trail—rewards include a lookout and a waterfall—to rejoin the Alouette Valley Trail at Mike Lake Road. A one-way trip is also possible, if you plan ahead and leave a second vehicle at the Spirea Nature Trail parking lot, close by to the east. Spirea is a short wheelchair-accessible loop that circles a wetland and offers interpretive panels in Chinese, English, French, and German.

The Alouette Valley Trail lies in the territories of the Katzie, Kwantlen, and Stó:lō peoples. No bikes, drones, fires, smoking, or vaping. Dogs must be on leash.

······················· **Fun Fact** ······················

The breathing hole on the right side of the slug's mantle (the fleshy lobe behind the head) is called the pneumostome.

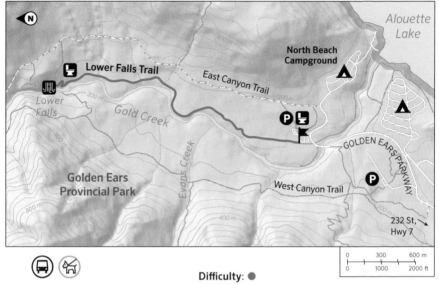

Distance: 5.7 km (3.5 mi)
Elevation gain: 115 m (380 ft)
High point: 260 m (850 ft)
Season: most of the year

Difficulty: ●
Quality: ☺ ☺ ☺
Map: Canadian Map Makers Golden Ears Provincial Park
Trailhead: 49°20'02" N, 122°27'28" W

YOU NEVER FORGET your first hike, right? For me, it's the Lower Falls Trail in Golden Ears Provincial Park. Near the end of Camp Snowfly (dubbed "Camp Rainfly" for obvious reasons), I and a gaggle of Burnaby boys followed a grizzled Scout leader to a waterfall on Gold Creek. Evidently, it made an impression on me. Judging by the scores of families that flock to it on weekends, I'm not the only one with warm feelings about this trail.

GETTING THERE

Transit: Parkbus offers coach service on summer weekends to the Gold Creek parking lot from Burrard Station in Vancouver.

Vehicle: Heading east on Highway 7 (Lougheed Highway) in Maple Ridge, turn left onto Dewdney Trunk Road, 5 km (3.1 mi) east of the Pitt River Bridge. (On Trans-Canada Highway 1, take Exit 57 in Surrey or Exit 58 in Langley. Follow signs for the Golden Ears Bridge, take the Maple Ridge exit, and continue onto Dewdney Trunk.) In 6 km (3.7 mi), make a left on 232 Street. At the traffic circle, go right on 132 Avenue/Fern Crescent. Stay on Fern, bear left onto 128 Avenue, and rejoin Fern, which becomes Golden Ears Parkway. Continue to the Gold Creek parking lot (toilet available) at parkway's end. The Golden Ears Provincial Park gate is closed 11 p.m. to 7 a.m. from April to mid-October, and 5:30 p.m. to 8 a.m. from mid-October to March.

THE HIKE

From the west side of the parking lot, descend to a trailhead kiosk. Strike off north on the Lower Falls Trail, following a wide gravel path into a lush rainforest of moss-covered western red cedars. Pass massive boulders and stumps surrounded by sword ferns. The first bit of uphill comes at the 500-m (0.3-mi) mark. The rushing waters of Gold Creek, on their way to Alouette Lake (sa'anəsaʔɬ xa'cɛʔ in hən̓q̓əmin̓əm̓, the language of the Katzie First Nation), are audible to your left.

After 1 km (0.6 mi), the trail pulls alongside the creek's left bank. During the rainy months, there are big puddles to jump in. Two leftward side paths—check out the big old cedar at the second entrance—provide access to a gravel point bar. In sunny weather, the beach is a fine spot to have a picnic or to cool your feet in the clear, sparkling water (which mesmerized me as a youngster). Keep kids close if they're playing at the water's edge—mind the current.

Continuing upstream, the trail rounds a cutbank with a point bar across the creek. It's a textbook example of fluvial deposition (inside bank) and erosion (outside bank) at a stream bend. Spy Edge Peak to west and Mount Nutt to the east. Cross a couple of small bridges en route to the 2-km (1.2-mi) marker. Huge hollow stumps present fun photo ops for little ones.

After the 2.5-km (1.6-mi) marker, find an outhouse on the right and an upstream-facing bench on the left. Head up the path to a viewpoint, 2.7 km (1.7 mi) in, to feel the mist and hear the roar of the powerful Lower Falls of Gold Creek. A sign (Waterfalls Are Dangerous!) on the

The Lower Falls of Gold Creek.
PHOTO: JOAN SEPTEMBRE

wooden fence warns you to stay away from the whitewater and slippery rocks. A plaque at the base of the bench here memorializes Sean Anthony Langille (1970–1991), who died working on a trail crew in the park.

You can turn around here or push on for 150 m (0.1 mi) to a second viewpoint to see the top of the Lower Falls. This trail section is more rugged, with rocks and roots to avoid tripping on. Keep kids behind the chain-link fence at trail's end (49°21′13″ N, 122°27′04″ W), despite a gap allowing passage.

Orange tapes opposite the start of the fence indicate a connector trail offering access to the East Canyon Trail and the possibility of a loop. However, this is a steep, rough route best left to experienced hikers and older kids. Accordingly, return to the trailhead via the Lower Falls Trail.

The trail lies in the territories of the Katzie and Stó:lō peoples. No bikes, drones, fires, smoking, or vaping. Dogs must be on leash.

·················· **Fun Fact** ··················

Panning for gold is not allowed at Gold Creek. Indeed, it's illegal in Golden Ears Provincial Park and other provincial parks. B.C. has 14 recreational panning reserves (one is on the Fraser River at Hope), where you can seek gold with a hand pan and shovel. Metal detectors are not permitted.

27 Railway Trail | Trail map on p. 121

Distance: 12 km (7.5 mi)
Elevation gain: 65 m (210 ft)
High point: 90 m (295 ft)
Season: all year

Difficulty: ●
Quality: ☺
Map: NTS 92-G/1 Mission
Trailhead: 49°11'58" N, 122°24'13" W

YOUR MISSION, should the kids choose to accept it: Navigate the west shore of the lower of two hydroelectric reservoirs on the Stave River and spot the remains of a historical B.C. Electric Railway line. A swimming beach awaits at trail's end.

GETTING THERE

Vehicle: From Highway 7 (Lougheed Highway) in Maple Ridge, go north on 287 Street, just west of the Stave River and Silvermere Lake. Continue onto Wilson Street and enter Mission. Turn right into the Railway Trail's upper parking lot, 4 km (2.5 mi) from the highway. Note: The gate closes a half-hour before dusk and when the lot fills up during peak hours.

THE HIKE

Mission's Railway Trail is located in the Hayward Lake Reservoir Recreation Area, part of B.C. Hydro's Stave River hydroelectric complex. Impounded by the Ruskin Dam, downstream of Stave Lake (šxʷey̓əqʷs in Halq'eméylem, the language of the Stó:lō people), Hayward Lake has filled a granite canyon in the heart of Kwantlen First Nation territory since the 1930s. Weather-beaten railway trestles recall the past, a version of which is highlighted by interpretive panels. During the early 1900s, electric trains ferried supplies to the powerhouse and community at Stave Falls and returned to the Canadian Pacific Railway station at Ruskin with cedar logs for local sawmills.

From the trailhead, drop down to the lakeshore and follow the wide gravel path northeast. Hikers and mountain bikers are cautioned against idling in the section of the Railway Trail around Bob Brook. Dramatic signs warn of landslide risk heightened by heavy precipitation, with the potential hazard rating ranging from low to extreme.

Pass a little beach. Debris booms float in the cloudy blue-green water. Blackberries are plentiful along the sun-baked path with power lines overhead. For young birders, the brown-headed cowbird, hairy woodpecker, killdeer, rufous hummingbird, violet-green swallow, and western tanager are common sights. At intervals, the trail curves up and away from the shore to bridge streams under the dappled light of Douglas-fir (ts'sa:yelhp in Halq'eméylem) and western red cedar (xpá:yelhp) trees.

After 5.5 km (3.4 mi) on the Railway Trail, leave the slide hazard zone and turn left onto Harry's Trail (49°13′11″ N, 122°21′38″ W). Round a pond, clockwise, in shade. At trail's end, continue straight past a large parking lot and the warden's house to the busy beach with sand, picnic tables, and toilets. After lunch and perhaps a swim (no lifeguards), head southwest on the Railway Trail for 5.7 km (3.5 mi) to return to the trailhead.

Fires, guns, hunting, motorized vehicles, and smoking are prohibited. Dogs must be leashed (and aren't allowed at the main beach). While the Railway Trail is shared with bikes, the Hayward Reservoir Trail (Steelhead Falls, Hike 28) on the east side of Hayward Lake is hiking-only.

Blackberries on the Railway Trail.

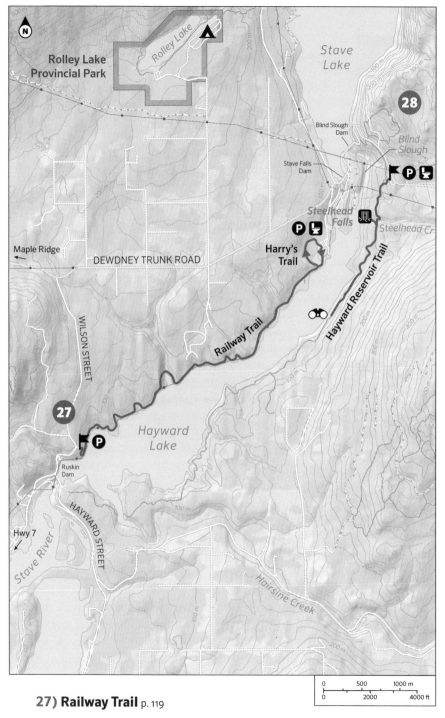

27) **Railway Trail** p. 119

28) **Steelhead Falls** p. 122

28 Steelhead Falls | Trail map on p. 121

Distance: 5 km (3.1 mi)
Elevation gain: 80 m (260 ft)
High point: 130 m (430 ft)
Season: all year

Difficulty: ●
Quality: ☺ ☺
Map: NTS 92-G/1 Mission
Trailhead: 49°13′47″ N, 122°20′52″ W

PLUNGING 20 M (65 FT) over three tiers, Steelhead Falls is a popular year-round destination for families in B.C. Hydro's Hayward Lake Reservoir Recreation Area. It's just one reason to take a forest hike on the Hayward Reservoir Trail, dawdling at viewpoints on the way.

GETTING THERE

Vehicle: From Highway 7 (Lougheed Highway) in Maple Ridge, go north on 287 Street, just west of the Stave River and Silvermere Lake. Continue onto Wilson Street and enter Mission. Turn right on Dewdney Trunk Road, 6 km (3.7 mi) from the highway. Cross the Stave Falls Dam and Blind Slough Dam; continue 1.3 km (0.8 mi) east. Turn right into the Hayward Reservoir Trail's small parking lot (toilet available). Note: The gate closes a half-hour before dusk and when the lot fills up during peak hours.

THE HIKE

The trailhead is the highest point of this outing, so be sure to save some energy for the hike out. From the kiosk, picnic table, and outhouse below the parking lot, go through the stile and descend the gravel path. Turn left at the next two junctions to join the 10-km (6.2-mi) Hayward Reservoir Trail on its journey south from the Blind Slough Dam to the Ruskin Dam. The former is one of two dams impounding Stave Lake (šxʷey̓əqʷs in Halq'eméylem, the language of the Stó:lō people), immediately upstream of Hayward Lake.

Pass a log bench as you amble in a lovely forest of Douglas-fir and western red cedar. Cross a power-line corridor and a charming wooden

Hayward Lake from the picnic table viewpoint.

bridge over Brown Creek. Mind the sheer drop on your right as you reach Steelhead Creek and its bridge. Go by a rotting bench and the Reservoir Trail's 3-km (1.9-mi) post.

After 800 m (0.5 mi) on foot, hang a hard right at the Steelhead Falls junction (49°13′29″ N, 122°21′00″ W). Descend a muddy path and wooden stairs for 150 m (0.1 mi) to the viewing box, with its soggy bench. See how long you can stand in the mist, first refreshing then bone-chilling. This destination will suffice for many kids.

However, to enjoy a longer nature break and quieter woods, keep going south on the Reservoir Trail. Try sitting on a seat fashioned out of a stump. Lots of small wooden bridges—a hit with preschoolers if my son is any indication—lie ahead on the gentle path. Go over Mark Creek and Duwaine Creek and by a mossy bench.

At the 4-km (2.5-mi) post, leave B.C. Hydro's recreation area and enter Mission Municipal Forest. The next boardwalk has steps and a bench in the middle of it. Point out all the big stumps with notches in them; historically, loggers wedged springboards into these notches and stood on the boards to cut a tree down.

The muddy trail descends gradually to a bridge just above the lakeshore, 1.5 km (0.9 mi) from the Steelhead Falls junction. In another 70 m (80 yd), spot a rotting picnic table to the right; this is our lakeside viewpoint destination (49°12′52″ N, 122°21′30″ W). Scan the sky

Little ones on the Hayward Reservoir Trail. PHOTO: ANDREA YOUNGHUSBAND

for bald eagles and the water for canoes, skip stones, and have a bite to eat. Look across Hayward Lake to the busy main beach and beyond to Mount Crickmer. Return the way you came.

Hayward Lake lies in the territories of the Kwantlen and Stó:lō peoples. While the Railway Trail (Hike 27) on the lake's west side is shared with mountain bikers, the Reservoir Trail is hiking-only. Fires, guns, hunting, motorized vehicles, and smoking are prohibited. Dogs must be leashed.

In recent history, steelhead—found in Hayward Lake—have been classified as a trout, then a salmon, and a trout again. Biologists now consider steelhead to be the anadromous (ocean-going) form of rainbow trout. In contrast, resident rainbow trout spend their whole lives in fresh water.

A stump seat on the Hayward Reservoir Trail.

Distance: 8 km (5 mi)
Elevation gain: 300 m (985 ft)
High point: 480 m (1,575 ft)
Season: all year

Difficulty: ■
Quality: ☺
Map: NTS 92-G/1 Mission, 92-G/8 Stave Lake
Trailhead: 49°13′45″ N, 122°20′14″ W

SEEK OUT a remnant of local history hidden in the woods. Spot fish breaking the surface of a placid lake. The Hoover Lake Trail beckons in Mission Municipal Forest, also known as Tree Farm Licence 26.

GETTING THERE

Vehicle: From Highway 7 (Lougheed Highway) in Maple Ridge, go north on 287 Street, just west of the Stave River and Silvermere Lake. Continue onto Wilson Street and enter Mission. Turn right on Dewdney Trunk Road, 6 km (3.7 mi) from the highway. Cross the Stave Falls Dam and Blind Slough Dam; continue 2 km (1.2 mi) east. Find the parking area on the north shoulder, opposite the Mission Landfill, also known as Minnie's Pit. Don't block the gate.

THE HIKE

From the yellow gate, head north on Hoover Road (HL 1000). Follow the gravel logging road left where a right branch bears a private property sign with an image of a gun. The main stem leads steadily uphill, keeping Brown Creek to your left. Cross a power-line corridor and service road (LH 300).

At Hoover Road's 1-km (0.6-mi) marker, fork left. (The right branch is signed HE 100.) Keep right where HL 100 exits left. Pass a clear-cut on your right at the 2-km (1.2-mi) marker. After HL 200 branches left, the main stem steepens briefly. Stay right at a fork with HL 300. After 3.1 km (1.9 mi) on foot, come to the signed start of the Hoover Lake Trail (49°15′13″ N, 122°19′53″ W) on the left, opposite a cutblock.

Ahead lies 900 m (0.6 mi) of wonderful, rooty single-track. Follow orange diamonds through a pleasant forest of western red cedars, Douglas-firs with bracket fungi, and mossy outcrops. The trail soon pulls alongside a historical corduroy logging road made of cedar planks. Please help preserve this remnant of the past by not straying off the designated path. Keep right at forks with diamonds in both directions. A boardwalk carries you over a pond.

After crossing the corduroy road, the trail descends, paralleling a creek to your left. Notice big stumps and rusted logging relics. (Leave No Trace principles discourage extracting or disturbing cultural artifacts and natural objects on public lands.) Arrive at the south shore of Hoover Lake.

Pause to take in the lake in its forested bowl. Then follow the trail left along the shore, treading a boardwalk over a wetland, and passing a small metal cross. Reach a quiet spot at the end of a peninsula (49°15′33″ N, 122°19′42″ W), with logs for sitting and a view of a little island in the middle of the lake. Cutthroat and rainbow trout ply these waters, which drain to nearby Stave Lake (šxʷeỷəqʷs in Halq'eméylem, the language of the Stó:lō people).

Hoover Lake lies in the territories of the Kwantlen and Stó:lō peoples. Camping and littering are prohibited, and dogs must be leashed in Mission Municipal Forest. Horses are restricted to logging roads.

If the kids have leftover energy to burn, try the Stave Dam Forest Interpretation Trail, 1.3 km (0.8 mi) west on the north side of Dewdney Trunk Road. Over 1.7 km (1.1 mi), the loop visits 10 stops designed to inform visitors about forestry practices.

30 ‹ Hicks Lake

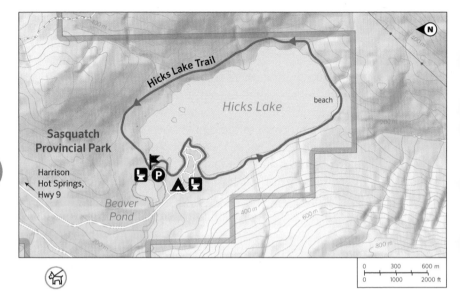

Distance: 6 km (3.7 mi)
Elevation gain: 45 m (150 ft)
High point: 245 m (800 ft)
Season: all year

Difficulty: ●
Quality: ☺
Map: NTS 92-H/5 Harrison Lake
Trailhead: 49°20'58" N, 121°42'25" W

BIGFOOT-SEEKING cryptozoologists quest for footprints, bones, and sightings in Sasquatch Provincial Park. Other similarly intrepid visitors hunt for hidden treasure in the second-growth cedar-hemlock woods. Good for a rainy day, the stroll around Hicks Lake is also ideal for introducing kids to the magical world of geocaching.

GETTING THERE

Vehicle: From Trans-Canada Highway 1 (Exit 135), east of Chilliwack—or Highway 7 (Lougheed Highway), west of Agassiz—head north on Highway 9 (Hot Springs Road) to Harrison Hot Springs. Go right on Lillooet Road, which turns into Rockwell Drive in 1 km (0.6 mi). After 5.2 km (3.2 mi) on Rockwell, take the right fork and enter Sasquatch

Provincial Park. Go right at the next fork onto a gravel road (2WD). Make a right at the Hicks Lake turnoff. Just before the campground, turn left to arrive at the day-use area (toilet available).

THE HIKE

For those harbouring the desire to cross paths with the yeti or other mysterious creatures, Sasquatch Provincial Park beckons in Kent, northeast of Harrison Hot Springs, and the territories of the Stó:lō and Sts'ailes First Nations. *Sasquatch* is an anglicization of the Halq'eméylem word Sa:sq'ets, which refers to the principal caretaker of Sts'ailes Xa'xa Temexw (sacred earth).

From the day-use area, set off south following the lakeshore. Sightings of Canada geese and salmonberries are probable, and barn swallows and red-breasted sapsuckers possible. The Hicks Lake Trail crosses a dam and fish ladder (cutthroat trout spawn in March and April) and skirts the Hicks Lake campground.

A sandy beach awaits at the lake's south end. Beware of swimmer's itch (cercarial dermatitis), a rash caused by parasitic schistosomes (flatworms). Look for rainbow trout jumping and for minnows and tadpoles along the lakeshore. Continue the counterclockwise loop on the east side of the lake. The Hicks Lake Trail eventually merges with a dirt road by the group campsite and delivers you back to the day-use area.

A wet spring hike in Sasquatch Provincial Park.

Canada goslings at Hicks Lake.

Several geocaches are stashed around the lake, which drains via Trout Lake Creek (Lhewálh in Halq'eméylem) into Harrison Lake (Peqwpa:qotel). Finding them requires a GPS (Global Positioning System) receiver loaded with geocache data or a smartphone with a geocaching app. Searching for geocaches (and their esoteric contents) in stumps, under tree roots, and along the lakeshore is both a frustrating and fun way to prolong this hike.

B.C. Parks' geocaching policy states: "Cache placement must not result in disturbing of soils, vegetation, wildlife or other natural or cultural heritage phenomenon." At Sasquatch Provincial Park, dogs must be leashed on trails. Hunting, smoking, and vaping are banned, as are fires outside of the campgrounds' fire rings.

······················· **Fun Fact** ·······················

Non-geocachers are called Muggles by geocaching enthusiasts. The term comes from J.K. Rowling's Harry Potter fantasy novels, in which a Muggle is a non-magical person. Geocaching started in 2000—when the first cache was placed in Oregon—three years after *Harry Potter and the Philosopher's Stone* was first published.

31 〈 **Mount Thom**

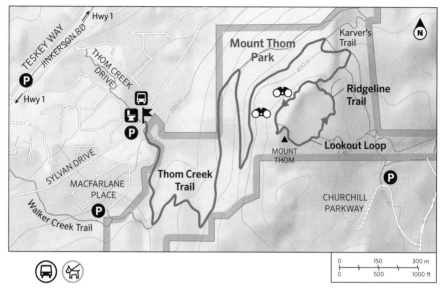

Distance: 7 km (4.3 mi)
Elevation gain: 290 m (950 ft)
High point: 484 m (1,590 ft)
Season: all year

Difficulty: ■
Quality: ☺ ☺
Map: Trail Ventures BC Chilliwack West
Trailhead: 49°06′16″ N, 121°55′11″ W

A FOOTHILL of the Skagit Range, Mount Thom is an enjoyable family-friendly hike in any season, including the fall, when the brilliant foliage shines yellow, orange, and red. Our lollipop hike climbs the mountain from Chilliwack's Promontory neighbourhood. On the summit, marvel at ravens soaring and diving overhead.

GETTING THERE

Transit: From Cottonwood Mall, take Chilliwack Transit Bus 4 (Promontory) to Sylvan Drive at Thom Creek Drive.

Vehicle: On Trans-Canada Highway 1 in Chilliwack, take Exit 123. Head south on Prest Road. Continue straight through two roundabouts onto

The view from Mount Thom. PHOTO: BRITTANY BRYDON

Teskey Way. Turn left on Jinkerson Road. Keep left at a private road. Go right on Thom Creek Drive. Turn right on Sylvan Drive and find street parking near the upper trailhead of the Thom Creek Trail (toilet available), 6.5 km (4 mi) from the highway.

THE HIKE

From the kiosk and water fountain on the southeast sidewalk of Sylvan Drive, enter Mount Thom Park and climb 130 numbered steps. Benches offer a chance to catch your breath. The viewpoint atop the stairs overlooks a suburban housing tract, the Fraser Valley, and Chilliwack Mountain (Qwemí:líts in Halq'eméylem, the language of the Stó:lō people). Follow the Thom Creek Trail into the mixed woods. A path from Mac-Farlane Place joins from the right.

Go left at the Walker Creek Trail junction and 1-km (0.6-mi) marker (in reference to the lower trailhead on Teskey Way). Zigzag steadily uphill on the wide gravel path. Watch out for Pacific banana slugs and sideband snails underfoot. Devil's club, lady fern, Oregon grape, stinging nettle, and thimbleberry grow under bigleaf maple, Douglas-fir, red alder, and western red cedar trees. Lose some elevation and pass the 2-km (1.2-mi) marker.

At the Summit Bypass Trail junction, go right. The trail dips again. Climb 22 unnumbered steps. A bench offers a rest and a partial viewpoint. Keep right at signposts for Karver's Trail, Churchill Parkway, and the Ridgeline Trail, joining the Lookout Loop. Stay on the main gravel path as shortcuts go right. Pass a bench viewpoint—a little preview of what's to come—and follow a wire fence.

Finally, head up an eroded path to the satisfying summit viewpoint (49°06′15″ N, 121°54′45″ W), 3.3 km (2.1 mi) from the trailhead. Gaze southwest through the fireweed to Cultus Lake (Swí:lhcha), Vedder Mountain (Qoqó:lem), and the Vedder River (Lhewá:lmel). However, the daring ravens are indubitably the stars of the show.

Continue left, turning right at a kiosk just downhill from the summit. Stroll among big old-growth Douglas-firs. Go left on the quiet Ridgeline Trail for some sweet single track. Skip the signed but overgrown viewpoint off to the right. Meet the Lookout Loop, closing the counterclockwise summit loop; turn right and retrace your steps to Sylvan Drive.

Mount Thom is officially named Mount Tom due to uncertainty about the provenance of the toponym. The park lies in the territory of the Stó:lō people, including the Ts'elxwéyeqw Tribe. No camping, drones, fires, fireworks, guns, hunting, littering, motorized vehicles, plant harvesting, or smoking. Dogs must be leashed and poop cleaned up. Horses are not permitted on the Thom Creek Trail below the Karver's Trail junction.

Fireweed at the summit viewpoint.

32 Three Bears | Trail map on p. 137

Distance: 2.3 km (1.4 mi)
Elevation gain: 50 m (165 ft)
High point: 380 m (1,250 ft)
Season: all year

Difficulty: ●
Quality: ☺ ☺ ☺
Map: NTS 92-H/4 Chilliwack
Trailhead: 49°08'56" N, 121°47'31" W

LOOKING FOR a fairy-tale hike guaranteed to be a hit with little ones? Make tracks to Chilliwack Community Forest in the Eastern Hillsides and take a ramble on Three Bears. Like a river on a floodplain, this delightful trail meanders through lovely woods, offering a relaxed grade and plenty of opportunities for snack breaks. Interpretive panels will engage inquisitive young minds.

GETTING THERE

Vehicle: On Trans-Canada Highway 1 in Chilliwack, take Exit 129 and head south on Annis Road. Quickly turn left on Hack Brown Road. In 1.4 km (0.9 mi), continue straight onto Nixon Road for 750 m (0.5 mi). Fork left for Allan Road, which turns to gravel (2WD). In 1.4 km (0.9 mi), turn right and continue up to the Chilliwack Community Forest parking lot (51642 Allan Road; toilet available).

THE HIKE

Chilliwack Community Forest, opened in 2016, features a variety of trails shared by hikers and mountain bikers. The trail network is built and maintained by the Chilliwack Park Society with support from the City of Chilliwack and the Fraser Valley Mountain Bike Association. The forest lies in the territory of the Stó:lō people, including the Pilalt Tribe, and a few of the trails have names in Halq'eméylem.

Our easy lollipop hike starts to the left of the entrance kiosk. Set off on a gravel path lined with fireweed and thimbleberries. Pass a bench and pause at an interpretive panel noting how the Stó:lō use the salmonberry to keep track of the timing of salmon runs.

An interpretive panel on Pí:txel.

At the first junction, head right on Pí:txel (pronounced "PEET-hyul" and meaning "salamander") to begin a counterclockwise loop. Fork left by a panel featuring facts about the Steller's jay, where the Canyon Loop leaves to the right. Go by a bench.

Take the right fork for Three Bears—a 1-km (0.6-mi) horseshoe that's nirvana for young children. Devil's club and lady ferns grow under big moss-covered western red cedars. Ring a bell hanging from a tree root, perhaps in unison with a distant train horn. Spot a whimsical face on a trunk. Encounter three little log seats—presumably for the name-sake ursids. (Where's Goldilocks?) Keep left on the wandering path at first, pass the descent into the black-diamond Swoop path, and follow the orange squares to do the full loop around the picnic area.

A four-way junction marks the end of Three Bears (49°08′46″ N, 121°47′46″ W). Go straight ahead to keep going counterclockwise on Pí:txel. A memorial bench sits next to a panel about black bears. Keep left to stay on Pí:txel at junctions with the Cholqthet (pronounced "cholk-THET" and meaning "Dropping in, like a bird falling out of the nest for the first time") and Slug paths. Linger on a wooden platform built by a school's woodworking class or at another bench to enjoy a drink of water and the verdant forest scene. Red elderberry and vanilla-leaf are prominent in the understory. Back at the first junction, go right to return to the trailhead.

A wooden platform, built by students, on the Pí:txel trail.

A face on a tree trunk.

Horses, littering, motorized vehicles, and smoking are prohibited in Chilliwack Community Forest, which is open dawn to dusk. Dogs should be under control at all times. Hikers and trail runners are advised to step aside for mountain bikers and to refrain from stopping in the middle of the trail. For a longer, more challenging outing, approach the forest on the Thaletel Trail (Hike 33) from Lexw Qwò:m Park.

···················· **Fun Fact** ·····················

Found in forests and on stream banks, devil's club is a tall, deciduous shrub with irritating yellow spines and bright red berries. Indigenous peoples from Alaska to Oregon value its medicinal and other uses. Try to avoid getting pricked by this member of the ginseng family.

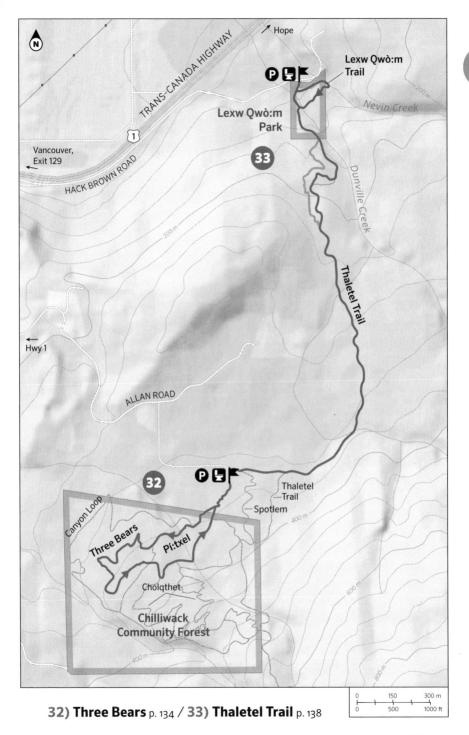

32) Three Bears p. 134 / **33) Thaletel Trail** p. 138

Distance: 5.4 km (3.4 mi)
Elevation gain: 250 m (820 ft)
High point: 335 m (1,100 ft)
Season: all year

Difficulty: ◆
Quality: ☺
Map: NTS 92-H/4 Chilliwack
Trailhead: 49°09′47″ N, 121°47′14″ W

THE THALETEL TRAIL winds its way through a lush forest of Douglas-firs and western red cedars, connecting Lexw Qwò:m Park and Chilliwack Community Forest in the Eastern Hillsides. The trail lies in the territory of the Stó:lō people, including the Pilalt Tribe. Interpretive signs teach visitors the pronunciation and English translation of trail names in the Halq'eméylem language. Old dams, crossed on bridges, add historical interest.

GETTING THERE

Vehicle: On Trans-Canada Highway 1 in Chilliwack, take Exit 129 and head south on Annis Road. Quickly turn left on Hack Brown Road. In 1.4 km (0.9 mi), make a left at the Nixon Road intersection to stay on Hack Brown. Pull into the parking lot at Lexw Qwò:m Park (51930 Hack Brown Road; toilet available), on the right, 3.5 km (2.2 mi) from the highway.

THE HIKE

In 2019, the City of Chilliwack opened Lexw Qwò:m Park in collaboration with the Chilliwack Park Society and Fraser Valley Mountain Bikers Association. Artist and herbalist Carrielynn Victor (Xémontélót) of the Cheam First Nation advised on the park's Halq'eméylem name, which is pronounced "luhw-KWOM" and means "always lots of moss."

Set off on the beginner-friendly Lexw Qwò:m Trail to the left of the map sign. The gravel path goes over Nevin Creek and then makes a 180-degree turn. Recross the creek upstream on a bridge over a 1950s intake formerly used by the Elk Creek Waterworks Company to supply

Lexw Qwo:m (luhw KWOM)

The traditional name for this area translates "always lots of moss". This descriptive term reminds us that this area of the mountain sees little sun and retains more moisture. A forest that is wet even during the hot summer is ideal for growing moss.

An interpretive sign in Lexw Qwò:m Park.

drinking water to Chilliwack. Watch water flow over the dam through the metal grate beneath your feet. Follow the path through majestic cedars and over the old Dunville Creek intake to the day-use area, with its picnic tables, bike repair station, and portable toilet, after 400 m (0.2 mi) on foot.

The Thaletel Trail begins left of the park information kiosk. (To the right is Thaletel's mountain-bike exit and the bottom of the Alhqéy path.) Thaletel, which is pronounced "THA-la-tell" and means "like a heart," refers to wild ginger. Hikers and trail runners are advised to let mountain bikers pass and to refrain from stopping in the middle of the trail. Follow the steep path up a ridge under cover of tall, mossy cedars and firs. Merge with the bike exit and keep left at the next junction.

Just past a log bench, fork right to avoid the Bolder Line downhill bike path. Keep left at the fork immediately above the top of Bolder Line. Ramps help bikers ride a log next to Thaletel. Pass the top of Alhqéy (pronounced "AL-th-key" and meaning "snake") and continue upward. Devil's club, lady ferns, and sword ferns grow in the understory.

Take plank bridges over a couple of creeks. With the trail getting increasingly muddier, fork left to bypass a skinny bridge for bikes. After the next plank bridge, the path becomes eroded and super slippery when wet. Keep sidehilling where the Magic bike path enters from the left. At a signed fork, go right on a 300-m (0.2-mi) hiking connector trail to end

The Thaletel Trail is shared by hikers and mountain bikers.

Bracket fungi on wood.

at a gravel road (49°08′58″ N, 121°47′30″ W), just below the Chilliwack Community Forest parking lot. The Spotlem (pronounced "SPOT-lum" and meaning "smoke") bike path emerges at this spot too.

To extend your hike, venture into the community forest and explore the Three Bears trail (Hike 32). Otherwise, head back down the Thaletel Trail to Lexw Qwò:m Park. (For a less-steep descent option toward the bottom, fork left onto Alhqéy and keep right at Chasing Squirrels.) Turn left at the day-use area to bypass the dams, return to the trailhead, and complete the reverse lollipop.

Dogs must be leashed in Lexw Qwò:m Park, which is open dawn to dusk. No camping, drones, fires, fireworks, guns, horses, hunting, littering, motorized vehicles, plant harvesting, or smoking.

34 Thacker Mountain

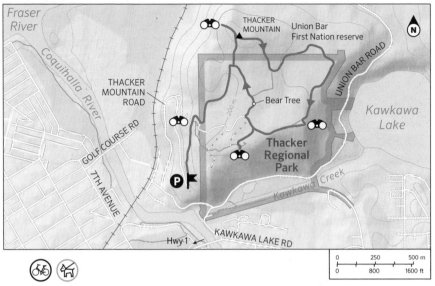

Distance: 4.8 km (3 mi)
Elevation gain: 130 m (430 ft)
High point: 240 m (790 ft)
Season: all year

Difficulty: ■
Quality: ☺ ☺
Map: NTS 92-H/6 Hope
Trailhead: 49°23'06" N, 121°25'33" W

THACKER MOUNTAIN rises east of the confluence of the Coquihalla River (Kw'ikw'iyá:la in Halq'eméylem, the language of the Stó:lō people) and Fraser River (Stó:lō) in Hope (Ts'qó:ls). A very pleasant lollipop hike takes in the views from all sides of this forested hill, formerly known as Little Mountain. Kids will be intrigued by the Bear Tree.

GETTING THERE

Vehicle: Heading east on Trans-Canada Highway 1, take Exit 170 in Hope. From the off-ramp, turn left. Under the highway overpass, go right on Old Hope Princeton Way. In 1 km (0.6 mi), make a left on 6th Avenue, followed by a right on Kawkawa Lake Road. After crossing the Coquihalla River, turn left on Union Bar Road, then make a sharp

Taking a break on a viewpoint bench. PHOTO: BRITTANY ZUROWSKI

left on Thacker Mountain Road. In 1.6 km (1 mi), park on the shoulder by the end of the paved road.

THE HIKE

From the cul-de-sac, start up the gravel service road. Keep left at a three-way junction under a rock wall and pass a yellow gate. Where a log lies by the roadside, a mossy bluff off to the left offers benches from which to admire the lovely view of little Landstrom Ridge (also known as Crack Mountain) and bigger Dog Mountain (Q'á:w in Halq'eméylem) behind Hope and the Coquihalla-Fraser confluence. Keep kids away from the edge.

Keep going up the road, which enters Thacker Regional Park and land owned by the University of British Columbia. After the road curves right, 500 m (0.3 mi) from your start, go left on a trail that rounds a wetland with a bridge over its outflow. Stay on the main trail as it bends right where a path with pink flagging tape leaves left.

Go left at a three-way junction, 500 m (0.3 mi) from the gravel road, to begin a clockwise loop. In 200 m (220 yd), detour left for a near-summit viewpoint (49°23′38″ N, 121°25′20″ W), with an outcrop for sitting and snacking, that affords another grand perspective of Hope, the Fraser Valley, and the Skagit Range. For a brief outing, turn around here, after 1.4 km (0.9 mi) on foot.

Continuing the loop, pass a big Douglas-fir, gradually descend, and merge with an old road coming from the right in 400 m (0.2 mi).

Walk the planks over the outlet of a wetland, spying Hope Mountain (St'ámiya) to the south. Encounter another big fir. Go left and up a side path, 1 km (0.6 mi) from the last junction, for a partial viewpoint (49°23'17" N, 121°24'54" W) overlooking Kawkawa Lake (Q'éwq'ewe). Ogilvie Peak (Qemqemó), Macleod Peak (Yusoló:luk), and Mount Outram provide the backdrop.

The side path quickly rejoins the main trail. Hit the gravel road, 400 m (0.2 mi) after the lake viewpoint. Turn left and head up to the 15-decibel-watt antenna tower (49°23'14" N, 121°25'16" W). Go around the barbed wire fence to score a big view of Hope Mountain from the clifftop. Kawkawa Creek (Sqw'íqw'x̱weq), home to kokanee salmon runs, empties into the Coquihalla River below.

The trailhead is 1.7 km (1.1 mi) away on our lollipop. Head back down the gravel road, passing your previous path on the right and a gate on the left, and turning right on another path, 300 m (0.2 mi) from the tower. By a pond, encounter the arboreal oddity called the Bear Tree by locals. Kids will be drawn to the little cave underneath the pair of seemingly conjoined trees. After 400 m (0.2 mi) on this path, turn left at a junction from earlier to close the clockwise loop. Retrace your steps to the gravel road and down to the trailhead.

Thacker Mountain lies in the territory of the Nlaka'pamux and Stó:lō peoples, including the Tiyt Tribe (encompassing the Chawathil, Peters, Popkum, Seabird Island, Shxw'ōwhámel, Skawahlook, Union Bar, and Yale First Nations). Fraser Valley Regional District bylaws prohibit camping, feeding wildlife, fires, fireworks, foraging, hunting, littering, motorized vehicles, remote-controlled devices (including drones), smoking, and vaping in regional parks. Dogs must be leashed and poop picked up. Stay on designated trails.

················· **Fun Fact** ·····················

Kokanee are the non-anadromous (landlocked) form of sockeye salmon. Whereas anadromous sockeye migrate from fresh water to ocean and back, kokanee spend their entire lives in rivers and lakes.

35 Little Douglas Lake

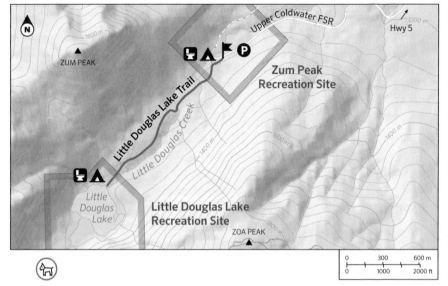

Distance: 3.2 km (2 mi)
Elevation gain: 90 m (295 ft)
High point: 1,310 m (4,300 ft)
Season: late spring to early fall

Difficulty: ■
Quality: ☺ ☺
Map: John Baldwin Coquihalla Summit
Trailhead: 49°38'26" N, 121°05'31" W

NESTLED IN a cirque between Zoa Peak and Zum Peak, north of Coquihalla Pass, Little Douglas Lake boasts glassy water and a striking backdrop. The short trail to the lake is ideal for an overnighter with young ones or packing in a stand-up paddleboard.

GETTING THERE

Vehicle: From its junction with Crowsnest Highway 3 (Hope-Princeton Highway), east of Hope, head north on Yellowhead Highway 5 (Coquihalla Highway) for 50 km (31 mi). After cresting the summit of Coquihalla Pass, take Exit 228 (Coquihalla Lakes Road). At the base of the off-ramp, turn left on Upper Coldwater Road. (The Britton Creek Rest Area is straight ahead.) Cross the highway on an overpass, go over a

Stand-up paddleboarding
at Little Douglas Lake.

cattle guard and a bridge, and pass a sand and gravel pit and highway maintenance yard. The road turns to narrow gravel (2WD, high clearance recommended), becoming Upper Coldwater Forest Service Road. Keep left at the gas pipeline markers early on. Ford a little creek. Stay right where two rough roads leave left. After 7 km (4.3 mi) on the FSR, park on the right shoulder, just before the Zum Peak Recreation Site (toilet available).

THE HIKE
Find the signed start of the Little Douglas Lake Trail on the south shoulder, just east of the Zum Peak Recreation Site and the bridge over Little Douglas Creek. Cross the ditch and follow orange diamonds into the woods. Quickly merge with a path (on the right) from the rec site, which features two roadside campsites and an outhouse.

Heading southwest, tread boardwalks over brooks and moist ground. The flora includes American speedwell, black huckleberry, corn lily, leatherleaf saxifrage, oak fern, and pink monkey-flower. Cross Little Douglas Creek to river left on logs and planks—hazardous in high water.

Switchback uphill, then resume the gentle ascent. Log-walk over a tributary. Arrive at the Little Douglas Lake Recreation Site, with its tent pads, outhouse, and food cache. A final section of boardwalk leads through a marsh and past a beaver dam at the outlet to a communal

The backcountry campground at Little Douglas Lake.

firepit and the muddy lakeshore (49°37′54″ N, 121°06′23″ W), 1.6 km (1 mi) from the trailhead.

Mirrored in the water, Zopkios Peak commands the head of the magnificent valley, which is lined with rock faces and rockslides. To the southeast, a waterfall plunges off Zoa Peak. Wildflowers—scarlet paintbrush, slender rein orchid, sticky false asphodel, and subalpine daisy—bloom in the lakeside marsh. Try to spot the beaver lodge across the lake.

Although the mosquitos may have you screaming bloody murder, if you opt for a swim, please don't pollute the freshwater ecosystem with insect repellent and sunscreen. Little Douglas Lake drains to the Salish Sea via Little Douglas Creek, and the Coldwater (Ntstlatko in Nłeʔkepmxcín, the language of the Nlaka'pamux people), Nicola, Thompson, and Fraser (Quoo.ooy) Rivers.

The Little Douglas Lake Trail is managed by Recreation Sites and Trails B.C., a branch of the Ministry of Forests, Lands, Natural Resource Operations and Rural Development. No fireworks, littering, motorized vehicles, shooting, tree cutting, or gatherings of 15 or more people. Dogs must be under control at all times. Please use the outhouses and practice Leave No Trace.

36 ‹ Similkameen Trail | Trail map on p. 151

Distance: 4.8 km (3 mi)
Elevation gain: 30 m (100 ft)
High point: 1,190 m (3,900 ft)
Season: late spring to early fall

Difficulty: ●
Quality: ☺
Map: Clark Geomatics 104 Manning Park
Trailhead: 49°03′49″ N, 120°47′52″ W

THE WESTERN SECTION of the Similkameen Trail in E.C. Manning Provincial Park is a pleasant ramble and ideal for young children. The wildflowers are brilliant in spring and summer, and so is the foliage in autumn. In winter, it's a great place to introduce kids to snowshoeing.

GETTING THERE

Vehicle: From Trans-Canada Highway 1 in Hope, head east on Crowsnest Highway 3 (Hope-Princeton Highway) for 66 km (41 mi). At the Manning Park Resort, turn right on Gibson Pass Road. In 1.2 km (0.7 mi), cross a bridge over the Similkameen River and find the Windy Joe/Pacific Crest Trail parking area on left side of the road.

THE HIKE

Start at the wooden Manning Park sign on the south side of the road. Immediately, fork left for the Similkameen Trail. (Right is the Little Muddy Trail to Twenty Minute Lake.) Arctic lupine, heart-leaved arnica, and spreading phlox burst forth with vibrant petals among downed trees in the open terrain. Shrubs of saskatoon, a type of serviceberry, bear fruit.

The multi-use trail, which stays on the right side of the Similkameen River, is shared with horse riders and mountain bikers (and crosscountry skiers in winter). Bikers yield the right-of-way to hikers; both give way to equestrians. Follow big orange reflective markers into the woods. Take bridges over streams, including Little Muddy Creek, and boardwalks over wet patches. Where the trail pulls alongside the

An old bridge on the Similkameen River.

Similkameen River, look for American dippers and harlequin ducks in the swift water.

A minor incline leads to the Windy Joe Trail junction, after 2.1 km (1.3 mi) on foot. Keep left to part ways with the Canadian extension of the long-distance Pacific Crest Trail. (Tell the kids that a right turn can take you to the Canada-U.S. border in 11 km [6.8 mi] and Mexico in a further 4,265 km [2,650 mi]—a five-month journey!)

Go east on a mellow double track. Scan the forest floor for common funnel and false morel mushrooms and dragon horn lichens. Plants include baneberry, Hooker's fairybells, oak fern, sand violet, showy Jacob's-ladder, star-flowered false Solomon's-seal, and western meadowrue.

Descend a muddy bit to a signposted junction. The Similkameen Trail turns right and continues east to Castle Creek on a rougher path that becomes terribly overgrown and beset by deadfall. However, keep left on the double track to arrive at a rusty old truss bridge on the Similkameen River (49°03′29″ N, 120°46′20″ W), 2.4 km (1.5 mi) from the trailhead. A sign warns that the trail beyond this point is closed due to flooding. There's also a hole in the middle of the bridge deck, which has no railings.

Locate a shady lunch spot under the trees immediately downstream of the bridge. It's best to keep kids out of the strong current. Rainbow trout and Dolly Varden ply these waters, which flow to the Pacific Ocean via the Okanogan River and the Columbia River, south of the border. The riparian zone is habitat for coastal tailed frogs and long-toed salamanders. Retrace your steps to the trailhead.

The Similkameen Trail lies in the territories of the Nlaka'pamux and Syilx peoples. The Similkameen Valley is home to the Nsyilxcən-speaking Sməlqmix people, represented by the Lower and Upper Similkameen Bands, from whom the river's anglicized name is derived. Drones, foraging, hunting, smoking, and vaping are prohibited. Dogs must be leashed.

If the kids and adults still have energy to burn, try the Canyon Nature Trail. The 2-km (1.2-mi) loop starts across Gibson Pass Road from the Windy Joe/Pacific Crest Trail parking area.

··········· **Fun Fact** ···········

Lichens are part fungus and part alga (a plant) or cyanobacterium (a bacteria). They live together and help each other. Some lichens look like mosses, which are plants.

Macrofungi beside the Similkameen Trail.

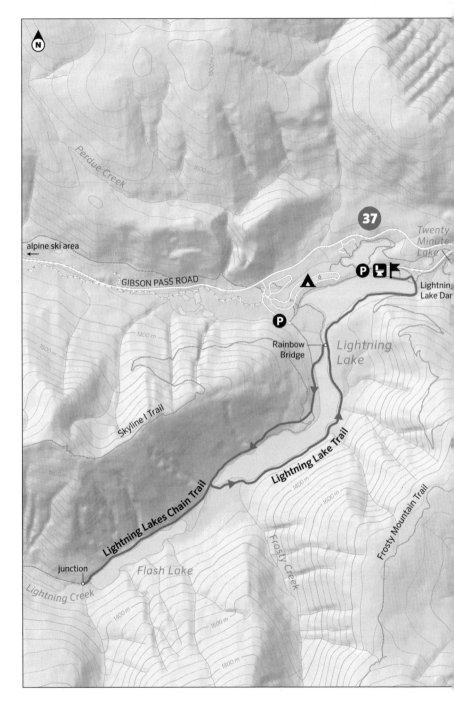

36) Similkameen Trail p. 147 / **37) Flash Lake** p. 152

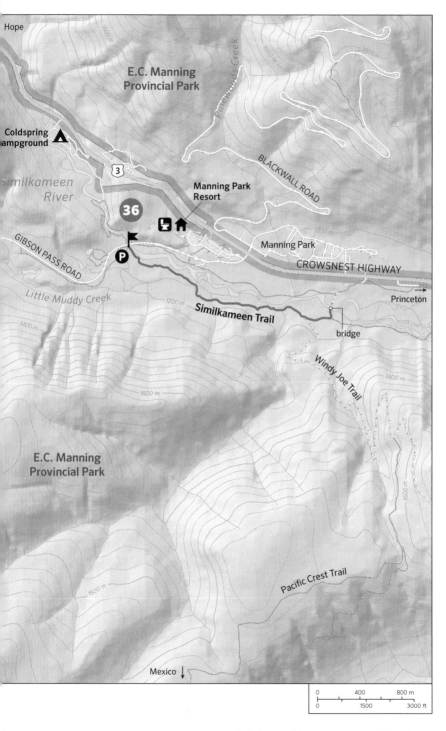

Hope

E.C. Manning
Provincial Park

Pinewoods Creek

Coldspring
Campground

3

Similkameen
River

BLACKWALL ROAD

36

Manning Park
Resort

Manning Park

GIBSON PASS ROAD

P

CROWSNEST HIGHWAY

Little Muddy Creek

Similkameen Trail

Princeton

bridge

Windy Joe Trail

E.C. Manning
Provincial Park

Pacific Crest Trail

Mexico ↓

0   400   800 m
0   1500   3000 ft

37 **Flash Lake** | Trail map on p. 150; photo on p. 6

Distance: 10 km (6.2 mi)
Elevation gain: 45 m (150 ft)
High point: 1,275 m (4,180 ft)
Season: late spring to early fall

Difficulty: ●
Quality: ☺ ☺
Map: Clark Geomatics 104 Manning Park
Trailhead: 49°03′44″ N, 120°49′39″ W

IT'S NO SECRET why hikers, canoeists, kayakers, and stand-up paddleboarders flock to Lightning Lake in E.C. Manning Provincial Park every summer. The full-featured campground is perfect for families, the lake holds rainbow trout, and the chilly bluish-green water makes for invigorating swimming. A less-ballyhooed reason to visit is the rodents, namely the squirrels, chipmunks, and beavers. Leave the crowd behind by setting out for Flash Lake.

GETTING THERE
Vehicle: From Trans-Canada Highway 1 in Hope, head east on Crowsnest Highway 3 (Hope-Princeton Highway) for 66 km (41 mi). At the Manning Park Resort, turn right on Gibson Pass Road. Turn left in 3 km (1.9 mi). Continue to the parking lot at the Lightning Lake day-use area (toilet available).

THE HIKE
The whistled calls and burrows of Columbian ground squirrels welcome you to the Lightning Lake day-use area. (Don't approach or feed wildlife, no matter how cute.) Start at the kiosk by the beach (no dogs allowed). Head east on the paved path and cross the 1960s-era dam at the end of the lake. The Frosty Mountain Trail quickly strikes off to the left. Stick with the easy Lightning Lake Trail to reach Rainbow Bridge, in 1.5 km (0.9 mi). Take the postcard-worthy bridge, made of glulam (glued laminated timber), over the lake's narrows.

On the other side, turn left and pass a bench (snack time?). Look for beaver-chewed trees along the shore and a beaver lodge across the water. Keep left where the Lightning Lake Trail meets the trail from the Spruce Bay parking lot (an alternative starting point). Stay on the wide, level trail, spurning a couple of side paths offering lakeshore access to the left and the start of the Skyline I Trail to the right. Baneberry, black huckleberry, saskatoon, tall Oregon-grape, and wild strawberry plants bear fruit in the understory.

Come to a junction (49°02′44″ N, 120°51′06″ W), 1.8 km (1.1 mi) from Rainbow Bridge. Here, the Lightning Lake Trail turns left, crossing a bridge over Lightning Creek immediately downstream of a beaver dam at the lake outlet. However, if energy and enthusiasm remain in good supply, continue southwest for 1.6 km (1 mi) on the Lightning Lakes Chain Trail to enjoy the quieter surrounds of Flash Lake.

Keep right at a signpost, where a log bridge spans Lightning Creek to the left as part of the closed Flash Lake Loop on the south side of the slender lake. Spot a beaver lodge across the water. Cross the base of a rockslide and pass a logjam at the foot of Flash Lake. Reach a junction (49°02′17″ N, 120°52′06″ W), with a bridge to the left, marking the downstream end of the Flash Lake Loop. Although the Lightning Lakes Chain Trail keeps going to Strike Lake, a backcountry campground (permit required), and Thunder Lake, this is an opportune spot for day-hiking families to turn around. Beyond this point, avalanches make the old trappers' path hazardous to travel in winter and early spring.

On the way back, turn right and cross the bridge at the Lightning Lake outlet. Follow the Lightning Lake Trail on the south shore for 3.7 km (2.3 mi), bypassing Rainbow Bridge, to return to the day-use area. Keep your eyes peeled for snowshoe hares (technically lagomorphs, not rodents) and three-toed woodpeckers among the amabilis fir, Douglas-fir, Engelmann spruce, and western white pine trees. Sightings of black bears and mule deer are common.

Manning Provincial Park lies in the territories of the Nlaka'pamux, Stó:lō, and Syilx peoples. In the Halq'eméylem language of the Stó:lō, the Lightning Lakes area is known as Skwa-kwa-eets. Dogs must be leashed, bikes and horses are prohibited on these trails, and fires are discouraged in the backcountry. No foraging, hunting, smoking, or vaping.

B.C.'s provincial parks are drone-free zones. Also known as unmanned aerial vehicles, drones cause noise pollution, stress wildlife, and disturb other park users, so they are illegal to operate without permission in provincial parks.

38 Dorman Point | Trail map on p. 156; photo on p. 2

Distance: 2.4 km (1.5 mi)
Elevation gain: 100 m (330 ft)
High point: 110 m (360 ft)
Season: all year

Difficulty: ■
Quality: ☺ ☺
Map: NTS 92-G/6 North Vancouver
Trailhead: 49°22'46" N, 123°20'01" W

LET'S BE HONEST: Half the fun of hiking on Bowen Island (Nex̱wlélex̱w-em in S̱k̲wx̲wú7mesh sníchim, the language of the Squamish Nation) is riding the *Queen of Capilano* ferry. Perfect for a mini adventure with the kids, the quick jaunt to Dorman Point pays off with potential sightings of bald eagles, turkey vultures, and vessels running B.C. Ferries' Horseshoe Bay–Departure Bay route. The hike is ideal for foot passengers and, conveniently, starts and finishes by an ice cream window.

GETTING THERE

Transit: Take TransLink Bus 250 (Horseshoe Bay), 257 (Horseshoe Bay Express), or 262 (Brunswick/Caulfeild) to the Horseshoe Bay ferry terminal.

Vehicle: From Vancouver, take Trans-Canada Highway 1 west to the B.C. Ferries terminal at Horseshoe Bay (Exit 3) in West Vancouver. Park in the long-term parking lot. (If you bring a vehicle to the island, park at the Snug Cove picnic area [toilet available], off Dorman Road.)

THE HIKE

At Horseshoe Bay (Ch'ax̱áy in S̱k̲wx̲wú7mesh sníchim), catch a sailing to Bowen Island. From the Snug Cove (Kwíl'ak̲m) ferry dock, walk 100 m (110 yd) west on Bowen Island Trunk Road to Cardena Road. At the war memorial opposite Cardena, head left on a boardwalk known as the Lady Alexandra Promenade. Pass by shops and benches, take the bridge over Davies Creek, and arrive at a Crippen Regional Park kiosk.

Go straight across the field at the Snug Cove picnic area to start up the hiking-only Dorman Point Trail, 300 m (0.2 mi) from the road. Follow the wide gravel path past a seemingly double-headed western red cedar. Quickly fork left, then right, in the mixed woods. Keep left at a wooden barrier. Zigzag up the slope, which supports Douglas-firs, lady ferns, Oregon grape, and salal. Ignore a right-hand path.

Emerge at the top of Robinson Road, 700 m (0.4 mi) from the picnic area. Go left at the signpost and tackle the final steep push to the Dorman Point viewpoint (49°22′40″ N, 123°19′33″ W), just 200 m (220 yd) farther. A sign warns of cliffs. The viewpoint is located on an outcrop of Bowen Island Group rock, dating back to the Jurassic Period and the age of the dinosaurs. Take a seat on a bench under an exfoliating arbutus tree.

Peer east over the treetops at St. Marks Summit, Mount Strachan, Black Mountain, Whyte Islet at Whytecliff Park (St'éx̱w't'ek̲w's), and Howe Sound (Átl'k̲a7tsem). A steep path to the right drops down to a bluff looking out at Queen Charlotte Channel, Point Grey (Elk̲sn), Passage Island (Smelhmelhéích), and Dorman Bay to the south. It's 1.2 km (0.7 mi) back to the trailhead—and ice cream.

No amplified sound, balloons, camping, drones, feeding wildlife, fires, flower or mushroom picking, motorized vehicles, smoking, or vaping in Crippen Regional Park. Dogs must be leashed. Parks Canada explored the possibility of adding land on Bowen Island, including Crippen, to Gulf Islands National Park Reserve. However, in 2011, Bowen Island voters rejected the idea in a referendum.

························· **Fun Fact** ·······················

A flock of raptors (birds of prey), such as turkey vultures, circling overhead and riding thermal updrafts is called a *kettle*. A group of vultures is a *committee* when perching in trees and a *wake* when feeding on a carcass.

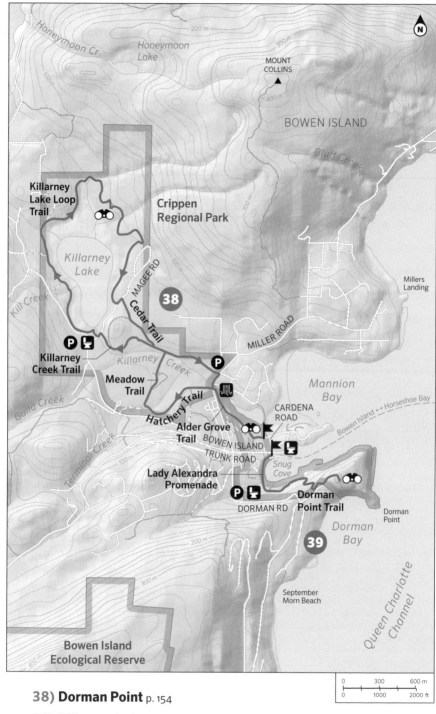

Honeymoon Cr

Honeymoon
Lake

200 m

300 m

MOUNT
COLLINS

400 m

BOWEN ISLAND

Bluff Creek

Killarney
Lake Loop
Trail

Crippen
Regional Park

Killarney
Lake

MAGEE RD

100 m

38

Millers
Landing

Cedar Trail

Kill Creek

MILLER ROAD

P

Killarney
Creek Trail

Killarney Creek

Mannion
Bay

Meadow
Trail

Hatchery Trail

Bowen Island ↔ Horseshoe Bay

Guild Creek

Alder Grove
Trail

BOWEN ISLAND
TRUNK ROAD

CARDENA
ROAD

Terminal Creek

Lady Alexandra
Promenade

100 m

Snug
Cove

Dorman
Point Trail

P

DORMAN RD

Dorman
Point

Dorman
Bay

39

200 m

Queen Charlotte Channel

300 m

September
Morn Beach

Bowen Island
Ecological Reserve

400 m

0   300   600 m
0   1000   2000 ft

38) Dorman Point p. 154

39) Killarney Lake p. 157

39 Killarney Lake

Distance: 8 km (5 mi)
Elevation gain: 60 m (200 ft)
High point: 70 m (230 ft)
Season: all year

Difficulty: ●
Quality: ☺ ☺ ☺
Map: NTS 92-G/6 North Vancouver
Trailhead: 49°22'50" N, 123°20'03" W

ONE OF MY favoured destinations for a father-son outing is Bowen Island (Nex̱wlélex̱wem in Sḵwx̱wú7mesh sníchim, the language of the Squamish Nation). The foot-passenger-friendly hike to Killarney Lake ticks a lot of boxes—buses, ferries, big trees, a waterfall, a fish ladder, a beaver dam, etc.—as far as my son's interests are concerned. Potential encounters with horses on the trail are something to get excited about too.

GETTING THERE

Transit: Take TransLink Bus 250 (Horseshoe Bay), 257 (Horseshoe Bay Express), or 262 (Brunswick/Caulfeild) to the Horseshoe Bay ferry terminal.

Vehicle: From Vancouver, take Trans-Canada Highway 1 west to the B.C. Ferries terminal at Horseshoe Bay (Exit 3) in West Vancouver. Park in the long-term parking lot. (If you bring a vehicle to the island, park at the Snug Cove picnic area [toilet available], off Dorman Road.)

THE HIKE

At Horseshoe Bay (Ch'ax̱áy in Sḵwx̱wú7mesh sníchim), catch a sailing to Bowen Island. From the Snug Cove (Kwíl'aḵm) ferry dock, walk 100 m (110 yd) west on Bowen Island Trunk Road and turn right on Cardena Road. Head past the Bowen Island Public Library and the visitor centre to find the Crippen Regional Park entrance on the left.

Set off northwest on the Alder Grove Trail. Moments later, detour right to take in the view of Deep Bay from the tranquil Bowen Island

Memorial Garden. Reach Bridal Veil Falls, 600 m (0.4 mi) from the trailhead. Drop down a path to the right to see the cascade and aging fish ladder on Killarney Creek.

At the end of Alder Grove, take the Miller Road crosswalk to begin the Hatchery Trail. Keep right at a signpost. Pass a hollow tree worth hiding in. Cross a bridge over Terminal Creek and head right on the Meadow Trail. Follow the path by benches and an equestrian ring, through Terminal Creek Meadows, and to a bridge over Killarney Creek, where a beaver dam raises the water level in a marsh. During my son's first visits to Bowen Island, we only made it as far as this lovely spot, 1.9 km (1.2 mi) from the trailhead. Blue dasher dragonflies flit among the blackberry shrubs, and Mount Gardner rises to the west.

Make a left on the Killarney Creek Trail to keep going to Killarney Lake, 800 m (0.5 mi) away. Listen for the rustling of garter snakes. Fork left at the Cedar Trail junction to begin a clockwise loop. Meet Magee Road, turn left, and recross Killarney Creek. Exit the gravel road to the right on the Killarney Lake Loop Trail.

Pause to observe the lily pads from a bench beside the Killarney Lake dam (49°23′18″ N, 123°21′15″ W). Head through a picnic area, passing an outhouse, and continue on the level loop trail. Cross a bridge on Kill Creek. Keep right at signposted junctions. In the lakehead marsh, a bench offers a rest stop on a boardwalk.

On the east side of the lake, the loop trail is more rugged and has its ups and downs. A bench viewpoint off to the right overlooks a beaver lodge. Follow the loop trail to Magee Road and briefly go left. Turn right on the Cedar Trail. Merge with the Killarney Creek Trail and stick with it to Miller Road. Go right to reunite with the Alder Grove Trail. Retrace your steps to Snug Cove to complete the double lollipop hike.

No amplified sound, balloons, camping, drones, feeding wildlife, fires, flower or mushroom picking, motorized vehicles, smoking, or vaping in Crippen Regional Park. Dogs must be leashed. According to Metro Vancouver regional parks' Canine Code of Conduct, folks with dogs should yield to other hikers.

Killarney Creek on Bowen Island (Nex̱wlélex̱wem).

The viewpoint at the Bowen Island Memorial Garden.

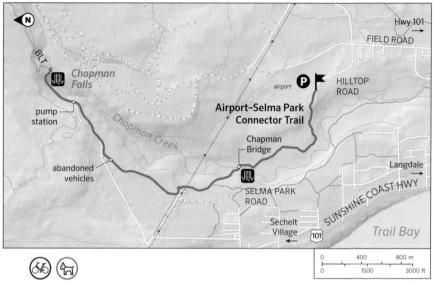

Distance: 9 km (5.6 mi)
Elevation gain: 120 m (390 ft)
High point: 160 m (525 ft)
Season: all year

Difficulty: ●
Quality: ☺ ☺ ☺
Map: NTS 92-G/5 Sechelt
Trailhead: 49°27′28″ N, 123°42′57″ W

WITH BRIDGES, waterfalls, and abandoned vehicles, a forest jaunt along Chapman Creek (ts'úḵw'um stulu in sháshíshálem, the language of the shíshálh Nation) in Sechelt (ch'átlich) is guaranteed to entertain kids of all ages. Aviation enthusiasts, young and old, will also enjoy plane spotting by the airport trailhead.

GETTING THERE

Vehicle: B.C. Ferries offers daily sailings between West Vancouver and the Sunshine Coast via the Horseshoe Bay–Langdale route. From the Langdale ferry terminal, take Highway 101 (Sunshine Coast Highway) northbound. In Sechelt, 2.8 km (1.7 mi) west of Roberts Creek Provincial Park, turn right (north) on Field Road. After 1.6 km (1 mi), go left

Moss-covered vehicles left in the woods.

One of the pipe bridges on the way to Chapman Falls.

The bridge over Chapman Creek (ts'úḵw'um stulu).

on Hilltop Road. (Straight ahead is Sunshine Coast Regional Airport's Gate 2, and right is Sechelt Wilson Forest Service Road.) Pull into the parking lot outside the airport's main gate (4536 Hilltop Road).

THE HIKE

Your hike begins on a section of the Suncoaster Trail. When completed, the Suncoaster Trail will run approximately 100 km (62 mi) from Earls Cove to Langdale, linking the ferry terminals and communities of the Lower Sunshine Coast.

Find the trailhead kiosk at the entrance to the parking lot. Open and close the gate; on the other side of the fence, immediately go right. The Airport–Selma Park Connector Trail leads past salmonberries and thimbleberries and down into a forest of birdsong. Be bear aware! Deer, spiny wood, and sword ferns flourish in the shade of lovely Douglas-firs and western red cedars. The wide path levels out and takes wooden bridges over several creeks.

At Chapman Bridge, 1.5 km (0.9 mi) from the airport, cross Chapman Creek to river right above a cascade. Signs caution against diving. The Chapman watershed supplies most of the Sunshine Coast Regional District's drinking water. The creek hosts runs of chum, coho, and pink salmon and steelhead trout. Go left and uphill at a map post. Shortly after, turn right on a wide, level path (49°28′02″ N, 123°43′44″ W) and leave the Airport–Selma Park Connector behind, 1.9 km (1.2 mi) from your start.

Head diagonally across a transmission corridor, perhaps spotting bald eagles circling high above or startling a garter snake underfoot. On the far side, ignore a road coming in from the right, then quickly turn right on the next double track to leave the buzzing high-voltage lines behind. Staying on the main path, reach the first of three rusty hulks. The abandoned sport-utility vehicle is followed by a moss-topped truck and station wagon, all slowly being reclaimed by nature. Picture time!

Continue northeast, bearing right twice to join a double track (49°28′36″ N, 123°43′30″ W) paralleling a second power-line corridor. Merge with the service road on your left. At the Chapman Creek Booster Pump Station, 3.9 km (2.4 mi) in, head straight onto a muddy road and into the woods. (A paved road goes left to a water treatment plant.) Pass old-growth Douglas-firs and listen to the creek grow louder as you continue upstream. Cross two curving pipe bridges, peering through the metal grates at the fern gullies beneath your feet.

Immediately after the second bridge, detour right at orange flagging for the unfenced Chapman Falls viewpoint. Tumbling over three tiers in a rainforest canyon, the waterfall is a powerful sight and sound. A plunging tributary joins the action. Hold on to kids and don't try to get close to the edge. A slip could have fatal consequences.

Keep going upstream to reach the final destination in short order (49°28′54″ N, 123°42′48″ W). Stick with the big water pipe where the BLT mountain-bike trail exits left. The tranquility of the narrow pool above the falls is in stark contrast to the turbulence below. Watch your step on the slippery rock. Keep kids away from the potentially treacherous water. Retrace your steps to the airport.

The Chapman Creek trails lie in the shíshálh Nation's ts'úḵw'um stulu kw'enit sim alap (Lower Chapman Creek Cultural Emphasis Area) and are shared by hikers and mountain bikers. No fires, horses, motorized vehicles, or smoking.

···················· **Fun Fact** ····················

A salmon nest is called a *redd*. After a spawning female salmon digs the shallow hole in the gravel bed of the river or lake where she was born and lays her eggs, a male salmon releases a cloud of milt to fertilize the eggs.

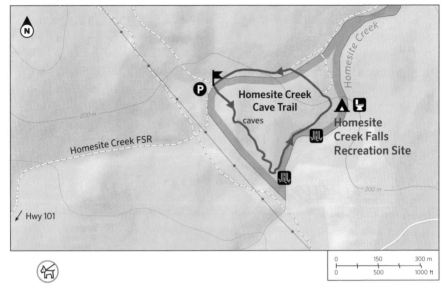

Distance: 1.4 km (0.9 mi)
Elevation gain: 40 m (130 ft)
High point: 210 m (690 ft)
Season: all year

Difficulty: ■
Quality: ☺ ☺
Map: NTS 92-G/12 Sechelt Inlet
Trailhead: 49°32'29" N, 123°55'11" W

WATERFALLS AND big trees and caves, oh my! Discover a hidden world of wonder on the shady Homesite Creek Cave Trail, near Secret Cove (stl'ítl'kwu in sháshíshálem, the language of the shíshálh Nation) on the Sechelt Peninsula.

GETTING THERE

Vehicle: B.C. Ferries offers daily sailings between West Vancouver and the Sunshine Coast via the Horseshoe Bay–Langdale route. From Sechelt Village, head north on Highway 101 (Sunshine Coast Highway) for 18 km (11 mi). After passing Stephens Way in Halfmoon Bay, as the highway curves left, turn right onto a gravel road (2WD). This is Homesite Creek Forest Service Road (Branch 1). Follow the main stem for

1.4 km (0.9 mi), across a power-line corridor, to find the signed day-use parking area on the left, opposite the trailhead.

THE HIKE

From the logging road, the rugged Homesite Creek Cave Trail leads southeast into the woods, with plenty of rocks and roots for little feet to negotiate. Douglas-firs and western red cedars—the latter being B.C.'s arboreal emblem—rise above sword ferns and dull Oregon-grape. Encounter the first of several tiny limestone caves under tree roots. By all means, take a closer look, but beware of unstable ground. Don't let kids venture inside the hollows.

You're treading on a karst landscape, where the dissolution of bedrock over millennia has created complex subterranean drainage systems. Famous karst areas include the Niagara Escarpment in Ontario and Mammoth Cave in Kentucky. Caves, dolines (sinkholes), and disappearing streams (spot one or two?) are characteristic features of this fascinating topography. To protect the sensitive environment, don't stray off the unmarked path, and to prevent injuries, avoid concealed openings. This isn't the place to play hide-and-go-seek.

Pull alongside a creek, then drop down by a pond and pass beneath a particularly majestic old-growth tree. The way forks as you close in

A waterfall on Homesite Creek.

An old-growth western red cedar on the Homesite Creek Cave Trail.

on Homesite Creek. Go left, but not before detouring straight ahead to visit the first cascade. Heading upstream, ignore a couple of side paths en route to the second waterfall.

From here, the trail quickly leads up and out of the woods to emerge at the Homesite Creek Falls Recreation Site by campsite 7 (49°32'26" N, 123°54'54" W). Amenities include a few pit toilets and, if a site is unoccupied, picnic tables. Dogs must be leashed.

It's 600 m (0.4 mi) farther to the day-use parking area. Follow the gravel road northeast and then northwest to exit the rustic campground and hit Homesite Creek FSR. Turn left and walk down the roadside to complete the counterclockwise loop. Watch out for logging trucks.

This hike pairs well with Pender Hill (Hike 42) or Skookumchuck Narrows (Hike 44) as part of a day or car-camping trip to the Sunshine Coast. For more family-friendly trails and waterfalls, stop at the Homesite Creek/Secret Cove Recreation Site on the west side of the Sunshine Coast Highway, just south of Homesite Creek FSR. Homesite Creek carries water from the Caren Range (spipiyus swiya in sháshíshálem) to the Long Arm of Secret Cove, and rears coho and chum salmon in its lower reaches.

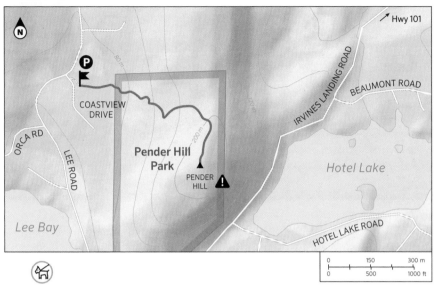

Distance: 1.6 km (1 mi)
Elevation gain: 170 m (560 ft)
High point: 234 m (770 ft)
Season: all year

Difficulty: ◆
Quality: ☺ ☺ ☺
Map: NTS 92-F/9 Texada Island
Trailhead: 49°38′32″ N, 124°03′41″ W

PENDER HILL is known as kw'enim ("looking") in sháshíshálem, the language of the shíshálh Nation. Fittingly, the sweeping views from the top will impress kids and adults alike. Pint-sized scrambly bits make the short and steep trail a fun challenge for the whole family.

GETTING THERE

Vehicle: B.C. Ferries offers daily sailings between West Vancouver and the Sunshine Coast via the Horseshoe Bay–Langdale route. From Sechelt Village, head north on Highway 101 (Sunshine Coast Highway) for 37 km (23 mi). By the gas station in Kleindale, turn left onto Garden Bay Road. In 5.4 km (3.4 mi), continue straight onto Irvines Landing Road, where Garden Bay bears left. After 3 km (1.9 mi), turn right onto

167

Looking out at Mount Daniel (shélkém) and Hotel Lake from Pender Hill (kw'enim). PHOTO: JOAN SEPTEMBRE

Lee Road. Make a right on Coastview Drive in 1 km (0.6 mi). Find the entrance to Pender Hill Park (4331 Coastview Drive) immediately on your left. Head up the gravel road to the tiny parking lot. Don't block the yellow gate.

THE HIKE

The trail starts to the left of the yellow gate and immediately crosses a little wooden bridge. Sword ferns line the gently rising path through the mixed woods. Cross a second bridge, accompanied by birdsong. In short order, the grade stiffens under the Douglas-fir and western red cedar trees.

A tree with a peculiar, zigzagging trunk offers a welcome excuse for a breather and photo op. See who can come up with the most fantastical explanation for the natural oddity. Mossy boulders and dull Oregon-grape cover the forest floor. Also referred to as Cascade barberry, the low-growing evergreen shrub has spiny leaves (ouch!), which turn red in autumn, and produces edible but sour fruit.

As it weaves uphill, the trail gets rockier. Little ones might need a hand clambering up and over the outcrops, which are slippery when wet. Stick to the main path, and don't cut switchbacks. Keep left at a fork with a shortcut. Head steeply up to gain the ridge. Follow the path as it bears right. Point out an arbutus tree, which is easily identified by its peeling cinnamon bark. Please don't deface these gorgeous tree trunks with your initials. Go up the final rise, joined from the right by the aforementioned shortcut.

Burst into the open on the summit (49°38′24″ N, 124°03′19″ W), with its bare and moss-covered rock. Continue forward a few steps for a grand perspective of the Malaspina Strait (sínkwu in sháshíshálem) and Salish Sea, and the lakes and islands of Pender Harbour (ḵálpilín). To the east, Hotel Lake lies at the foot of Pender Hill. Mount Daniel (shélkém) and Cecil Hill (wah-wey-we'-lath) stand like sentinels over the harbour.

Keep kids close and stick to established paths as you explore the bluffs. Scan the air for bald eagles and the ground for northern alligator lizards. The hilltop is also home to shore pine and wildflowers, such as chocolate lily and nodding onion. Watch your footing as you retrace your steps to the trailhead.

No amplified music, camping, fires, hunting, littering, or smoking in Pender Hill Park. Dogs must be leashed. Pender Hill lies in the shíshálh Nation's ḵálpilín–stséxwena kw'enit sim alap (Pender Harbour–Sakinaw Cultural Emphasis Area).

···················· **Fun Fact** ····················

The arbutus, or Pacific madrone, is an evergreen tree that's often found on rocky bluffs and in clearings within 8 km (5 mi) of the ocean in southwestern B.C. It has big green leaves, peeling red bark, and can grow up to 30 m (100 ft) tall. That's as high as three telephone poles stacked on top of each other!

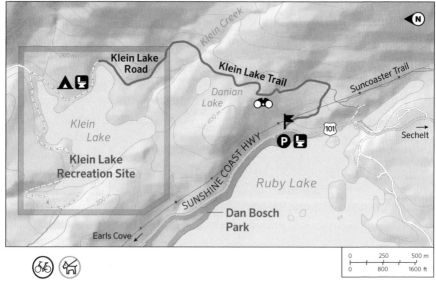

Distance: 6.5 km (4 mi)
Elevation gain: 150 m (490 ft)
High point: 190 m (620 ft)
Season: all year

Difficulty: ■
Quality: ☺ ☺
Map: NTS 92-G/12 Sechelt Inlet
Trailhead: 49°43'01" N, 123°58'06" W

EVER SAT ON a bench made of snowboards? Tackle the traverse from Ruby Lake to Klein Lake in the Pender Harbour (ḵálpilín in sháshíshálem, the language of the shíshálh Nation) area and tick this item off the family bucket list. Swimming holes at both ends of the hike make it easy to cool off on a hot day.

GETTING THERE

Vehicle: B.C. Ferries offers daily sailings between West Vancouver and the Sunshine Coast via the Horseshoe Bay–Langdale route. From Sechelt Village, head north on Highway 101 (Sunshine Coast Highway) for 48 km (30 mi). Turn left (west) into the Dan Bosch Park parking lot (toilet available), 5.5 km (3.4 mi) south of the Earls Cove ferry terminal.

THE HIKE

The Ruby Lake–Klein Lake traverse follows the Klein Lake Trail section of the Suncoaster Trail, a link in the National Hiking Trail. Your starting point, Dan Bosch Park, features a sandy beach and picnic area on the shore of Ruby Lake. However, the trailhead lies across the Sunshine Coast Highway, 70 m (76 yd) south. Watch out for traffic when crossing the roadway.

From the Suncoaster Trail kiosk on the east side of the highway, take the gravel road past a yellow gate and diagonally across a power-line corridor. Fork left at a map post, where the road to the right is gated, transferring from Suncoaster spur to mainline. In early summer, the roadside is alive with the purple and white blooms of common foxglove (taller than an adult), as well as common St. John's-wort, self-heal, Sitka columbine, and tiger lily. Follow the road under a power line—spy Ruby Lake below and raptors soaring above—and straight onto a path into the woods.

The trail zigzags sharply, before a brief paved section leads onto an open bluff (160 m/525 ft; 49°43′05″ N, 123°57′55″ W), 1.2 km (0.7 mi) from the trailhead. A big boulder sits under a Douglas-fir, and arbutus trees show off their flaking bark. Two benches, with snowboards for seats and backrests, look out over Ruby Lake and beyond to Cecil Hill

The east end of Klein Lake.

(wah-wey-we'-lath in sháshíshálem) and Mount Daniel (shélkém). For an abbreviated outing with ample payoff, turn around here after a snack. Just up the trail sits an enigmatic wooden statue. Bear left at the next map post. Skip a dreadfully overgrown side path that descends left to nearby Danian Lake (which a faded sign identifies as a clothing-optional area). Your route, an old logging road, crosses Klein Creek. Sword ferns and Siberian miner's-lettuce line this flat section. Gently rise to the high point at a junction with a kiosk and map post, after 2.4 km (1.5 mi) on foot.

Turn left to gradually descend via Klein Lake Road (North Lake Forest Service Road, Branch 2) to the day's destination. Watch out for 4×4 vehicles and dirt bikes in this section, and mountain bikes throughout. Pass a couple of yellow signs, warning that the road you came down is deactivated, to find a quiet little spot on the left where you can access the east end of the lake (140 m/460 ft; 49°43′46″ N, 123°57′43″ W). Encountering a map post and bird boxes along the treed lakeshore indicates you've gone farther. Unless you've arranged to be picked up at the lake, retrace your steps to the trailhead after lunch.

Outhouses are available a wee bit down the road at the Klein Lake Recreation Site's busy campground. Numerous docks facilitate swimming and canoeing. The lake provides habitat for the red-listed Pacific coast population of the western painted turtle. No fires, shooting, or smoking. Dogs must be leashed.

Klein Lake, also locally known as Killarney Lake, is drained by Klein Creek, which empties into Ruby Lake. The fresh water then flows via Sakinaw Lake (stséxwena) and Ruby Creek into Agamemnon Channel (lílkw'émin). All three lakes lie in the shíshálh Nation's ḵálpilín–stséxwena kw'enit sim alap (Pender Harbour–Sakinaw Cultural Emphasis Area), which contains the First Nation's main winter village sites.

delivers you quickly to North Point; right goes a tad farther to Roland Point.

During the ebb (outgoing) tide, head to North Point to see dramatic whirlpools form as water rushes out of Sechelt Inlet (ʔálhtulich), through Skookumchuck Narrows, and into Jervis Inlet (lékw'émin). A wooden bench sits in an open rocky area. A fence keeps visitors back from the treacherous current, which can surpass 30 km/h (16 knots). In winter, look for sea ducks called surf scoters in the water.

Roland Point is the place to watch the flood (incoming) tide. If you're lucky, you'll witness whitewater kayakers surfing the standing wave that forms. Hunt for crabs, sea stars, and urchins in the tide pools—but leave what you find. Keep kids away from the turbulent water. When you're done admiring the rapids—or slack water if you didn't time it right—retrace your steps to Egmont Road.

Skookumchuck Narrows Provincial Park lies in the shíshálh Nation's stl'íkwu kw'enit sim alap (Skookumchuck Narrows Cultural Emphasis Area). No bikes, camping, fires, motorized vehicles, smoking, or vaping. Dogs must be leashed and poop packed out.

························ **Fun Fact** ························

Skookumchuck means "strong water" in Chinuk Wawa, the intertribal and interethnic trade language of the Pacific Northwest. Indigenous peoples spoke the language first and European colonizers added to it and changed it, so Chinuk Wawa includes words from Chinookan, Salishan, and other Indigenous languages, Nootka Jargon (a simplified form of Nuučaańuł), English, and French.

45 Gray Peninsula

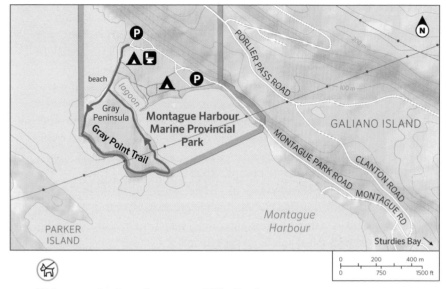

Distance: 2.2 km (1.4 mi)
Elevation gain: 40 m (130 ft)
High point: 40 m (130 ft)
Season: all year

Difficulty: ●
Quality: ☺ ☺ ☺
Map: NTS 92-B/14 Mayne Island
Trailhead: 48°54'00" N, 123°24'25" W

MONTAGUE HARBOUR is an ancestral village site known as Sum'nuw' ("inside place") to the Hul'qumi'num Mustimuhw (Hul'q'umi'num'-speaking people). The Gray Peninsula, a tied island protecting the harbour, offers a quick and easy hike that leads to lovely beaches and tide pools—perfect for young ones. It's found in Montague Harbour Marine Provincial Park on Galiano Island, a stop for kayakers paddling the Salish Sea Marine Trail.

GETTING THERE

Vehicle: B.C. Ferries offers daily service between Tsawwassen and Galiano Island. From the Sturdies Bay ferry dock, head northwest on Sturdies Bay Road for 2.7 km (1.7 mi). Keep left at the Porlier Pass Road intersection to continue onto Georgeson Bay Road. In 1.2 km (0.7 mi), turn right on Montague Road. Bear right onto Montague Park Road and enter Montague Harbour Marine Provincial Park, 8 km (5 mi) from the ferry dock. Keep right to reach the parking area at the far end of the car campground (toilet available). The park gate is closed between 11 p.m. and 7 a.m.

THE HIKE

Find the start of the Gray Point Trail by the boat launch. Commence the lollipop hike by heading south—between the outhouses, up the wide path, and along a wooden fence atop a cliff with great big arbutus trees. Descend stairs with a bench at the bottom. Take the path on the tombolo (sandy isthmus) straight ahead, with a tidal lagoon on your left and a white shell beach on the right that affords spectacular sunsets. Look for great blue herons.

The beach is one of several middens in Montague Harbour Marine Provincial Park. These archaeological deposits, which contain animal remains, charcoal, fire-cracked rocks, and stone artifacts, are protected by B.C.'s Heritage Conservation Act. Visitors are asked to refrain from touching or removing sea life and shells—clams, mussels, oysters, sea snails, etc.—and to return overturned rocks to their original position.

Re-enter the woods at the south end of the tombolo, after 300 m (0.2 mi) on foot. Fork right to begin a counterclockwise loop on the tied island. Hike through salal and beneath Douglas-firs and western red cedars. Admire the sedimentary rock shelf below to the right. Fences guard drop-offs.

Descend steps to a mini promontory, rising between two beaches, with a Montague Harbour Marine Provincial Park sign facing the water, 600 m (0.4 mi) from the trailhead. Charles Island lies northwest in Trincomali Channel, and Sutil Mountain rises to the southeast. Overhead power lines link Galiano Island and Parker Island (Qwi'qwuns in the Hul'q'umi'num' language).

Continue southeast on the forest path along the Gray Peninsula's outer shore, with 1.6 km (1 mi) remaining in the lollipop. Little ones can squeeze into a hollow arbutus tree. Benches and another marine park sign beckon at viewpoints along the way. Count the sailboats moored in Montague Harbour (where I first saw bioluminescent algae while on a Gulf Islands backpacking trip with Burnaby North Secondary School's

Boats off the
Gray Peninsula.

Outdoors Club). Keep left as you approach the lagoon, then go right to
return to the tombolo and the trailhead.

Montague Harbour is an 'A'lu'xut (resource harvesting) area for the
Hul'qumi'num Treaty Group, and also lies in the territories of the Hwlitsum, Stz'uminus, Tsawwassen, and W̱SÁNEĆ First Nations. Established
in 1959, B.C.'s oldest provincial marine park preserves a pocket of the
moist maritime coastal Douglas-fir biogeoclimatic subzone.

Drones, smoking, and vaping are prohibited in the park. No camping,
fires, or mountain biking on the Gray Point Trail. Dogs must be leashed
and are not allowed on beaches. In summer, a free shuttle offers daily
evening service between the Hummingbird Pub (47 Sturdies Bay Road)
and the park.

46 ⟨ **Pebble Beach** | Trail map on p. 183

Distance: 6.5 km (4 mi)
Elevation gain: 75 m (250 ft)
High point: 75 m (250 ft)
Season: all year

Difficulty: ■
Quality: ☺ ☺ ☺
Map: NTS 92-B/14 Mayne Island
Trailhead: 48°56′35″ N, 123°30′04″ W

PEBBLE BEACH is a pocket full of sunshine—or at least Salish Sea coastline—on Galiano Island. It's easy to lose yourself combing the surf for colourful stones and searching tide pools for burrowing green anemones. Starting from Galiano's main thoroughfare, this hike traverses the island's narrowest point to its eastern shore, following in the footsteps of generations of the Hul'qumi'num Mustimuhw (Hul'q'umi'num'-speaking people).

GETTING THERE

Vehicle: B.C. Ferries offers daily service between Tsawwassen and Galiano Island. From the Sturdies Bay ferry dock, head northwest on Sturdies Bay Road for 2.7 km (1.7 mi). Go right on Porlier Pass Road. In 1.7 km (1.1 mi), keep left at the Galiano Way intersection to stay on Porlier Pass. Turn left for Shore Access 31 (Zilwood Road) at 13755 Porlier Pass Road, 16 km (9.9 mi) from the ferry dock. Find parking space for a couple of cars immediately on the right. (The nearest public toilet is located at 25 Retreat Cove Road, beside the fire hall.)

THE HIKE

At Shore Access 31, a short trail leads southwest to a beach at the mouth of Grieg Creek on Retreat Cove (Xetthequm in the Hul'q'umi'num' language). However, our lollipop hike begins on the opposite shoulder of Porlier Pass Road, 40 m (44 yd) northwest. Carefully cross the road, find the Bell Trail sign, and head up into the woods.

Quickly, turn right at the Red-Legged Frog Trail junction. Tackle a brief steep section and pass a waterlogged pit. Follow the rippling path

179

Sandstone tide pools at Pebble Beach.

through blackberries, horsetails, Oregon grape, salal, big sword ferns, and tall Douglas-firs and onto an old road. Watch out for Pacific banana slugs underfoot. The old bridge over Grieg Creek is closed, so bear left to hit Vineyard Way, after 700 m (0.4 mi) on foot.

Turn right and briefly head up the paved road. (It's worth detouring left to visit Laughlin Lake, the largest freshwater body on Galiano Island. According to an interpretive kiosk, it's a stopover for migrating trumpeter swans.) Spot a yellow gate on the right and take the dirt road behind it, immediately bearing right to go by the other side of the Grieg Creek bridge and a gravel storage area. If turkey vultures are active in the vicinity, it might indicate the presence of a deer carcass in a nearby roadkill pit. Continue southeast on the Laughlin Trail, ducking under logs and going through a boulder blockade.

Arrive at the Pebble Beach Reserve (48°56′35″ N, 123°29′27″ W) at the end of McCoskrie Road, 1.8 km (1.1 mi) from the start of the Bell Trail. (For a shorter-and-sweet hike, park here.) Beginning a 3-km (1.9-mi) counterclockwise loop, head east on Sitka Lane and pass a rope gate.

In 700 m (0.4 mi), turn left on the Pebble Beach Trail (no bikes). Weave through the forest—the site of post-logging ecological restoration efforts by the Galiano Conservancy Association—descending gradually. Potential wildlife sightings include brown creepers, Columbian black-tailed deer, pileated woodpeckers, red-legged frogs, and rough-skinned newts. With the salt water visible through the trees ahead, go right at a junction. Step over logs and onto Pebble Beach (48°56′55″ N, 123°28′47″ W), 1.5 km (0.9 mi) from the nature reserve's entrance.

The view extends across the Strait of Georgia to the mountains of the Sunshine Coast and Lower Mainland. The wave-sculpted sandstone shelves on either side of the small beach are covered in rockweed and sea lettuce and contain tide pools awaiting curious eyes. Share the following tips for protecting life in the intertidal zone with the kids: Stand and walk on bare rock or sand rather than living organisms; don't poke or pick up creatures; keep dogs, insect repellent, hand sanitizer, and sunscreen out of tide pools; and help pack out any trash you find.

Backtrack to the previous junction. Go 650 m (0.4 mi) west on the Cable Bay to Pebble Beach Trail, following the most established path. It's a gorgeous stretch of mature coastal forest. At Cable Bay, emerge on an outcrop and hop onto the beach. Spot a no-anchor sign that warns of an underwater fibre-optic cable; re-enter the woods to the left of it. Ascend the straightforward Cable Bay Trail and return to the Pebble Beach Reserve entrance. Turn right and take the Laughlin Trail and Bell Trail back to Porlier Pass Road.

Managed by the Galiano Conservancy Association, the Pebble Beach Reserve lies in the territories of the Hul'qumi'num Treaty Group, and the Hwlitsum, Stz'uminus, Tsawwassen, and W̱SÁNEĆ First Nations. No camping, fires, or hunting.

·························· **Fun Fact** ······················

Galiano Island is named for Dionisio Alcalá-Galiano (1762– 1805), a Spanish naval officer who led an expedition during the 1790s to the B.C. coast in search of the Northwest Passage. Like other colonizers, Spanish explorers gave many places names to "claim" them. Other Spanish names in the Pacific Northwest include the Juan de Fuca Strait, Port Alberni, and Tofino.

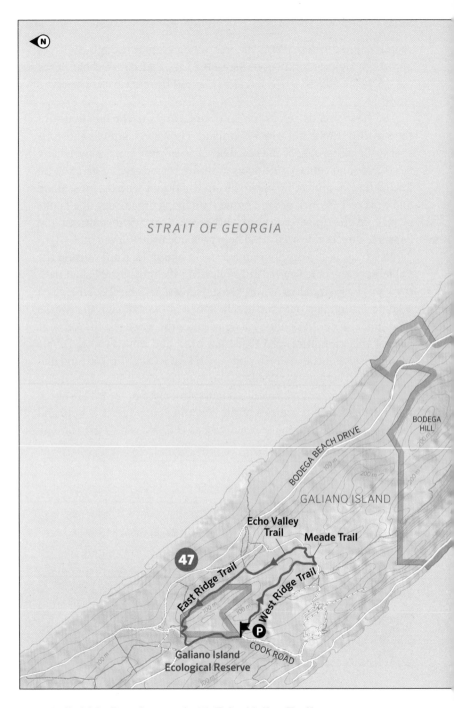

STRAIT OF GEORGIA

BODEGA HILL

BODEGA BEACH DRIVE

GALIANO ISLAND

Echo Valley Trail

Meade Trail

47

East Ridge Trail

West Ridge Trail

P

COOK ROAD

Galiano Island
Ecological Reserve

46) Pebble Beach p. 179 / **47) Echo Valley Trail** p. 184

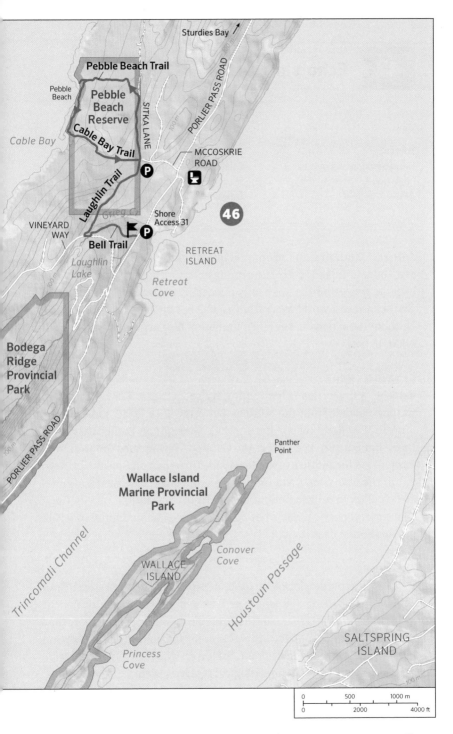

Sturdies Bay

Pebble Beach Trail

Pebble
Beach

PORLIER PASS ROAD

Pebble
Beach
Reserve

SITKA LANE

Cable Bay Trail

Cable Bay

MCCOSKRIE
ROAD

Laughlin Trail

Greg Co

P

46

VINEYARD
WAY

Shore
Access 31

Bell Trail

RETREAT
ISLAND

Laughlin
Lake

Retreat
Cove

Bodega
Ridge
Provincial
Park

PORLIER PASS ROAD

Panther
Point

Wallace Island
Marine Provincial
Park

Trincomali Channel

Conover
Cove

WALLACE
ISLAND

Houstoun Passage

SALTSPRING
ISLAND

Princess
Cove

0		500		1000 m
0		2000		4000 ft

47 Echo Valley Trail | Trail map on p. 182

Distance: 4.2 km (2.6 mi)
Elevation gain: 65 m (210 ft)
High point: 130 m (430 ft)
Season: all year

Difficulty: ●
Quality: ☺ ☺
Map: NTS 92-B/13 Duncan
Trailhead: 48°58′46″ N, 123°33′28″ W

CIRCUMAMBULATE an uncommon bog on the wooded ridges of northern Galiano Island. Introduce youngsters to the peeling bark of the arbutus tree. With the quiet only pierced by birdsong, the Echo Valley Trail can feel a world away from island hot spots such as Montague Harbour (Sum'nuw' in the Hul'q'umi'num' language) and Sturdies Bay (Shxixnetun).

GETTING THERE

Vehicle: B.C. Ferries offers daily service between Tsawwassen and Galiano Island. From the Sturdies Bay ferry dock, head northwest on Sturdies Bay Road for 2.7 km (1.7 mi). Go right on Porlier Pass Road. In 1.7 km (1.1 mi), keep left at the Galiano Way intersection to stay on Porlier Pass for another 17 km (10.6 mi). Turn right on Cook Road. Keep left at the Manastee Road intersection and trade pavement for gravel (2WD). Park in a little pullout on the right, 750 m (0.5 mi) up Cook. (The nearest public toilet is beside the North Galiano Community Hall [22790 Porlier Pass Road].)

THE HIKE

This quaint counterclockwise loop incorporates the West Ridge Trail, Echo Valley Trail, and most of the East Ridge Trail, north of Bodega Ridge. It enters the Galiano Island Ecological Reserve, one of more than 150 provincially designated areas that enjoy the highest level of environmental protection available in B.C. Biodiversity, science, and education are the raisons d'être of the ecological reserve system.

From the Jane's Crossing kiosk beside Cook Road, take the bridge over a pond. Head southeast on the West Ridge Trail in the dappled light. The gentle dirt path is lined with salal, sword ferns, Douglas-firs, and western red cedars. At 700 m (0.4 mi), keep left at a flagged fork. Dragonflies flit about a clearing with tansy ragwort, an invasive species from Europe.

The main path bears right at a fork, after 1 km (0.6 mi) on foot, then merges with a road entering from the right. Wooden signs mark the junction of the West Ridge Trail and Meade Trail. Turn left on Meade, a wide double track. After the Bodega Back Trail leaves to the right, take the left fork.

Quickly, spot the signed start of the Echo Valley Trail on the left. Follow the lovely old road across a wooded slope, with a depression below to the left. Admire the cinnamon-red (older) and greenish (younger) bark of arbutus trees.

Hit a four-way junction (48°58′44″ N, 123°32′53″ W), 1.2 km (0.7 mi) after leaving the West Ridge Trail. Straight ahead, the Winnie Trail leads to Bodega Beach Drive. However, turn left on the East Ridge Trail, another old road. Follow the blue tapes northwest, encountering evergreen huckleberries. After the Lyla Trail enters from the right, go left at a T-junction. Descend on single track to skirt the edge of the peat bog, with its ericaceous (acidic-soil-loving) shrubs and sphagnum moss, and pass a ruin.

After 1.1 km (0.7 mi) on the East Ridge Trail, go left on a gravel road and pass a yellow gate, with 900 m (0.6 mi) remaining in the loop. Make a left on Cook Road to return to Jane's Crossing. Look for great blue herons in the bog.

The Galiano Island Ecological Reserve lies in the territories of the Hul'qumi'num Treaty Group, including the Penelakut Tribe, and the Hwlitsum, Stz'uminus, Tsawwassen, and W̱SÁNEĆ First Nations. No camping, fires, fishing, foraging, hunting, motorized vehicles, or mountain biking. Dogs should be leashed. The Galiano Trails Society deserves credit for arranging trail access and maintenance on provincial land and, through easements, private property.

48 ‹ McKenzie Bight (W̱MÍYEȽEN̲)

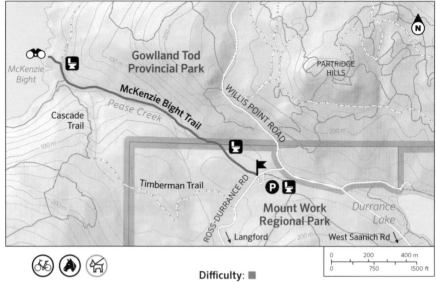

Distance: 3 km (1.9 mi)
Elevation gain: 150 m (490 ft)
High point: 150 m (490 ft)
Season: all year

Difficulty: ■
Quality: ☺ ☺ ☺
Map: NTS 92-B/11 Sidney, 92-B/12
Shawnigan Lake
Trailhead: 48°33'00" N, 123°29'26" W

LOCATED IN Gowlland Tod Provincial Park on Vancouver Island, the McKenzie Bight Trail heads down a lush rainforest ravine to the east shore of Saanich Inlet. Lively tide pools and lovely arbutus trees await. The hike is short and sweet, but you could easily while away most of day exploring the coastline.

GETTING THERE

Vehicle: B.C. Ferries offers frequent sailings between Delta and North Saanich via the busy Tsawwassen–Swartz Bay route. From the Swartz Bay ferry terminal, head south on Highway 17 (Patricia Bay Highway) for 14 km (8.7 mi) to Central Saanich. Turn right on Island View Road and left on Saanich Cross Road, which merges with Central Saanich

Road. Go right on Keating Cross Road for 2.6 km (1.6 mi) and left on West Saanich Road (formerly Highway 17A) for 3.7 km (2.3 mi). In Saanich, turn right on Wallace Drive, then go left on Willis Point Road for 4 km (2.5 mi). Make a left on Ross-Durrance Road to enter Highlands and find Mount Work Regional Park's parking lot on the left (toilet available). The gate is open sunrise to sunset.

THE HIKE

A big sign indicates the way to Gowlland Tod Provincial Park across the road from the parking lot. Set off on the wide McKenzie Bight Trail, quickly bearing right at the next set of signs. Pass an outhouse. Transfer from regional to provincial parkland at a boundary post.

Hike northwest and steadily downhill along the verdant ravine of Pease Creek. Lady, northern maiden-hair, and sword ferns, as well as Oregon grape, salal, salmonberry, stinging nettle, thimbleberry, three-leaved foamflower, and vanilla-leaf, thrive in the understory beneath mossy Douglas-fir and western cedar trees. Enjoy the birdsong and the soothing burble of flowing water.

Emerge from the temperate rainforest at the (sometimes dry) mouth of Pease Creek on McKenzie Bight (W̱MÍYEȾEN̲ ["place of deer"] in

The McKenzie Bight Trail in Gowlland Tod Provincial Park.

The rocky shore of McKenzie Bight (W̱MÍYEȻEN).

SENĆOŦEN, the language of the W̱SÁNEĆ people), formerly known as Camp Bight. A left-hand path crosses a bridge and links to the Cascade Trail, which, via the Timberman Trail, offers a more challenging approach. However, explore the beach ahead before following the trail to the right and up a little hill. Turn left at the outhouse to arrive on a grassy promontory with arbutus trees (48°33′19″ N, 123°30′21″ W), 1.5 km (0.9 mi) from the trailhead. Pull out the picnic you remembered to pack.

From this corner of Squally Reach, enjoy gorgeous views of Saanich Inlet in both directions. The hills of the Warwick Range and Malahat Ridge rise across the water and Saltspring Island (Klaathem in the Hul'q'umi'num' language, ĆUÁN in SENĆOŦEN) to the north. Look closely at the seashore; it's alive with acorn barnacles, ochre stars, crabs, mussels, and oysters. The onshore flora is colourful too, including broad-leaved stonecrop, Menzies' larkspur, and sea blush.

To prevent excessive whining, save some treats for the uphill return—via the same route—to the trailhead. The McKenzie Bight Trail is shared with horse riders and mountain bikers. Bikers yield to hikers; both give away to equestrians.

Gowlland Tod Provincial Park lies in the territories of the Malahat and W̱SÁNEĆ First Nations. No camping, drones, fires, smoking, or vaping. Dogs must be leashed, but B.C. Parks recommends pets be left at home. Take nothing but photographs; leave nothing but footprints.

49 ◀ Sooke Potholes (KWL-UCHUN)

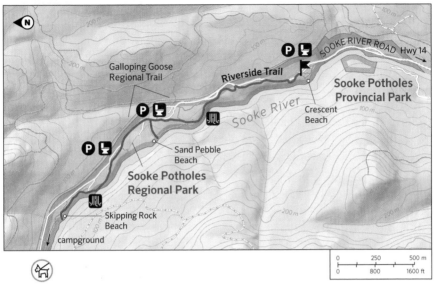

Distance: 4.2 km (2.6 mi)
Elevation gain: 60 m (200 ft)
High point: 90 m (295 ft)
Season: all year

Difficulty: ●
Quality: ☺ ☺ ☺
Map: NTS 92-B/5 Sooke
Trailhead: 48°25′56″ N, 123°42′51″ W

THE SOOKE POTHOLES, known to the T'Sou-ke Nation as KWL-UCHUN (Spring Salmon Place) in the SENĆOŦEN language, are simply out of this world. Take a hike on the Riverside Trail, cool off on one of the beaches, watch salmon returning to spawn, and marvel at the dramatic cliffs, swirl holes, and waterfalls created by the Sooke River on Vancouver Island.

GETTING THERE

Vehicle: B.C. Ferries offers frequent sailings between Delta and North Saanich via the busy Tsawwassen–Swartz Bay route. From the Swartz Bay ferry terminal, head south on Highway 17 (Patricia Bay Highway) for 25 km (16 mi) to Saanich. Take Exit 7 and go right on McKenzie Avenue for 1.8 km (1.1 mi). Use the right lane to join northbound Trans-Canada Highway 1 for 11 km (6.8 mi). In Langford, go left on West Shore Parkway for 4.2 km (2.6 mi). Turn right on Highway 14 (Sooke Road) and drive 16 km (9.9 mi) west to Sooke. Go right on Sooke River Road for 5.5 km (3.4 mi). Pass through Sooke Potholes Provincial Park (no potholes here), enter Sooke Potholes Regional Park, and pull into Parking Lot 1 (toilet available; pay parking in effect). The gate is open sunrise to sunset.

THE HIKE

Head past the toilets and up the stairs to the right to start the Riverside Trail. Quickly earn the day's first viewpoint, overlooking deep pools in the Sooke River gorge, with Crescent Beach downstream. Briefly walk along Sooke River Road (on the same side as oncoming traffic), then exit on a wide gravel path to the left. After pulling back alongside the road at a metal railing, follow the trail left to a pair of picnic tables.

Don't join the Victoria-to-Sooke Galloping Goose Regional Trail, loved by cycle tourers, across the road. Keep left to see the ruins, guarded by a barbed wire fence, of an abandoned lodge started in the 1980s. This viewing area is closed due to rockslides. Follow the fence north. Then bear left to descend to a junction where the Riverside Trail goes up the stairs to the right, after 800 m (0.5 mi) on foot. Detour straight ahead and down the rock stairs to the fenced viewing platforms. Peer over two waterfall tiers and down the gorge.

Continue upstream on the main path. (Side paths may lead to hazardous terrain.) Fork left by Parking Lot 2. Return to the road. At a pedestrian crossing, leave the road, and follow Mary Vine Creek left to Sand Pebble Beach. It's an excellent spot to have a picnic, go for a swim, or watch American dippers hunt for insects and fish in the river. Common harebell, common woolly sunflower, and Nootka rose bloom near the shore.

Backtrack to the road and walk north on the shoulder, passing a maintenance yard, to reach Parking Lot 3. At the north end, take the Riverside Trail left. Up the main path, rainwater fills puddles on a rocky clifftop that serves as a phenomenal viewpoint for the Sooke Potholes, formerly known as Devil's Potholes. Two deep pools are divided by a narrow, medieval-looking gap in the gorge. Keep kids away from the edge and beware of slippery rock.

Just upstream on the trail, by a picnic table and bike rack, another spectacular viewpoint stops you in your tracks. The erosive power of the river has carved a peculiar, almost nightmarish canyon out of the sandstone bedrock of the Sooke Hills. There are waterfalls, tight chasms, and swirl holes.

Push on upstream to another picnic table and bike rack. Take a side path left to Skipping Rock Beach (48°26'46" N, 123°43'35" W), 2.1 km (1.3 mi) from your start. Indeed, the flat stones are perfect for skimming.

The Riverside Trail continues upstream to Ripple Rock Beach, Hideaway Beach, and the Spring Salmon Place (KWL-UCHUN) Campground, operated by the T'Sou-ke Nation, 4.5 km (2.8 mi) from Parking Lot 1. However, Skipping Rock Beach is a suitable spot to turn around and retrace your steps downstream.

Administered by the Capital Regional District, Sooke Potholes Regional Park lies in the territories of the Sc'ianew, T'Sou-ke, and W̱SÁNEĆ First Nations. No camping, fires, flower picking, littering, motorized vehicles, or smoking. Dogs must be leashed.

Sooke Potholes Regional Park is part of the Sea to Sea Green Blue Belt, a planned corridor of contiguous protected areas from the Sooke Basin to Saanich Inlet. Other protected areas in the corridor include Sea to Sea Regional Park and Sooke Hills Wilderness Regional Park.

····················· **Fun Fact** ·····················

The world record for skipping stones is 88 skips in a row, set in 2013 by Kurt Steiner at Red Bridge in Allegheny National Forest, Pennsylvania.

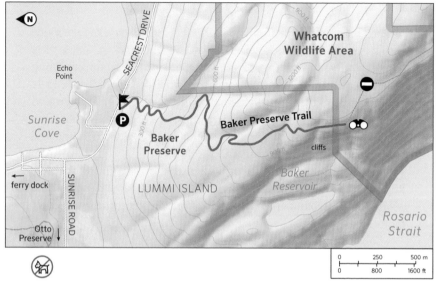

Distance: 5.3 km (3.3 mi)
Elevation gain: 310 m (1,020 ft)
High point: 350 m (1,150 ft)
Season: all year

Difficulty: ◆
Quality: ☺ ☺
Map: USGS Lummi Island
Trailhead: 48°41′40″ N, 122°39′43″ W

ALL ABOARD! Take the little ferry to Lummi Island for a mini adventure. Hike to an overlook on Lummi Peak for a splendid view of the San Juan Islands. Separated from the archipelago by the Rosario Strait, the island known as Smemiekw in Xwlemi'chosen, the language of the Lummi Nation, is just the ticket for a fun day trip.

GETTING THERE

Vehicle: Whatcom County's Lummi Island Ferry offers daily sailings. On Interstate 5, 25 km (16 mi) south of the Canada-U.S. border, take Exit 260 in Ferndale. Head west on Slater Road for 5.7 km (3.5 mi). Turn left on Haxton Way and continue south for 10.4 km (6.5 mi), through two traffic circles and onto Lummi View Drive, in the Lummi Reservation.

At Gooseberry Point, join the ferry lineup on the right and buy a ticket. Board the *Whatcom Chief* (crossing time: 5 minutes). From the Lummi Island ferry dock (toilet available), go left on South Nugent Road for 900 m (0.6 mi). Turn left on Seacrest Drive and continue for 2.8 km (1.7 mi). Pull into the Baker Preserve's small parking lot on the right.

THE HIKE

Visitors to the Baker Preserve, owned by the Lummi Island Heritage Trust, are required to sign in at the trail register. After doing so, start up the Baker Preserve Trail, with a little dam on the creek to your left.

The first part is very steep, but the 20 per cent grade doesn't last long. Oregon grape, northern maiden-hair fern, salal, and twinflower thrive at the feet of tall Douglas-fir trees in the second-growth forest. Orange jelly fungus brightens up the deadwood.

Hit a T-junction at the 1-mi (1.6-km) post. Go left on the double track. Pass a ravine and wetland as the road gradually snakes up the mountainside. The way levels out on Lummi Peak's northwestern flank, and a sign warns of dangerous cliffs on the right.

Finally, a sign directs you right to the overlook. The summit lies a distance southeast, but there's no public access on the road beyond this

A fence guards the cliff at the Lummi Peak overlook.

point. A brief path leads to a grassy bald atop an escarpment (320 m/ 1,050 ft; 48°40′53″ N, 122°39′48″ W), after 2.6 km (1.6 mi) on foot.

Look out over the Rosario Strait to Mount Constitution on Orcas Island (Swalex in Xwlemi'chosen) and the other isles of the transboundary Salish Sea—or just enjoy the clouds. An outcrop offers a lovely spot to sit and lunch, and a wooden fence guards the cliff, where a tall Douglas-fir is living on the edge.

The overlook is located outside of the Baker Preserve in the Whatcom Wildlife Area, which is administered by the Washington Department of Fish and Wildlife. The Lummi Island unit of the wildlife area was created to protect eyries of the peregrine falcon, formerly an endangered species.

Head back the very pleasant way you came. If you'd like to add an easy nature walk or two before catching a return ferry, visit the Otto Preserve (3560 Sunrise Road) or Curry Preserve (2449 North Nugent Road). Both nature preserves are also managed by the Lummi Island Heritage Trust.

The trust asks Baker Preserve visitors to limit groups to six people, stay on the trail, and adhere to Leave No Trace practices. A sign at the trailhead explains why it's a dog-free zone: "Whether their explorations lead them to accidentally step into an active bird nest, or to follow an irresistible scent into an animal's hiding spot, it doesn't take long for the sweetest or most well-behaved dog to inflict lasting damage to a local ecosystem." No bikes, drones, camping, fires, guns, horses, mushroom picking, or smoking.

················· **Fun Fact** ·····················

The Salish Sea encompasses the Strait of Georgia, Juan de Fuca Strait, and Puget Sound. A Western Washington University professor first proposed this name in 1989, and Coast Salish tribes and First Nations started using it. Washington State approved the new name in 2009 and the B.C. government in 2010.

51 ◀ Chuckanut Falls | Trail map on p. 197

Distance: 3.8 km (2.4 mi)
Elevation gain: 100 m (330 ft)
High point: 125 m (410 ft)
Season: all year

Difficulty: ■
Quality: ☺
Map: Square One Chuckanut Recreation Area
Trailhead: 48°42′03″ N, 122°29′21″ W

OLD-GROWTH TREES, a huge boulder, and two waterfalls? A hike to Chuckanut Falls in Bellingham offers plenty of interest to kids. It's just one of the many family-friendly outings possible in the superb trail network of the Chuckanut Mountains.

GETTING THERE

Vehicle: On Interstate 5 in Bellingham, 41 km (25 mi) south of the Canada-U.S. border, take Exit 250. Head west on State Route 11 (Old Fairhaven Parkway). Sticking with SR 11, turn left on 12th Street and bear left onto Chuckanut Drive. Continue south for 2.1 km (1.3 mi). Turn left into the parking lot at the North Chuckanut Mountain trailhead (toilet available).

THE HIKE

From the trailhead in the City of Bellingham's Arroyo Park, head south on a gravel path lined with sword ferns and over a boardwalk. In 200 m (220 yd), turn left on the Interurban Trail, a rails-to-trails link in the cross-border Coast Millennium Trail. Fork left at the No Horses Beyond This Point sign to bypass California Street. Cross Arroyo Creek on a bridge below a small cascade in the mixed woods.

At a junction with a map, go right and switchback uphill under big, old-growth Douglas-firs. Look up, kids! Take a right at the next junction and pass a glacial erratic. Enter Chuckanut Mountain Park, which is administered by Whatcom County.

After 1.3 km (0.8 mi) on foot, go left on the Chuckanut Falls Trail and left again on the Chuckanut Falls Viewpoint Trail. Descend the weaving

Chuckanut Falls on Chuckanut Creek (Chúkwenet).

path toward the din of Interstate 5. Douglas-firs and western red cedars tower over you. The path veers upstream as you near Chuckanut Creek (Chúkwenet in Xws7ámeshqen, the language of the Samish Nation). Spurn a path going left to private property.

Finally, arrive at Chuckanut Falls (48°41′53″ N, 122°28′17″ W), 1.9 km (1.2 mi) from the trailhead. Enjoy the sight and sound of the tall, narrow cascade—from safely behind the wooden fence. Take advantage of the bench. A sign advises you to stay on the trail so as to not disturb a restoration area. Chum and coho salmon and steelhead trout hatch, spawn, and die in the Chuckanut Creek basin.

Head back the way you came. Look for the fruiting bodies of false chanterelles in summer and autumn. Potential wildlife sightings include Columbian black-tailed deer and coyotes. Consider combining Chuckanut Falls with Teddy Bear Cove (Hike 52); just go left when you come to the Interurban Trail junction near the trailhead.

Dogs must be leashed in Chuckanut Mountain Park. No littering, shooting, or smoking.

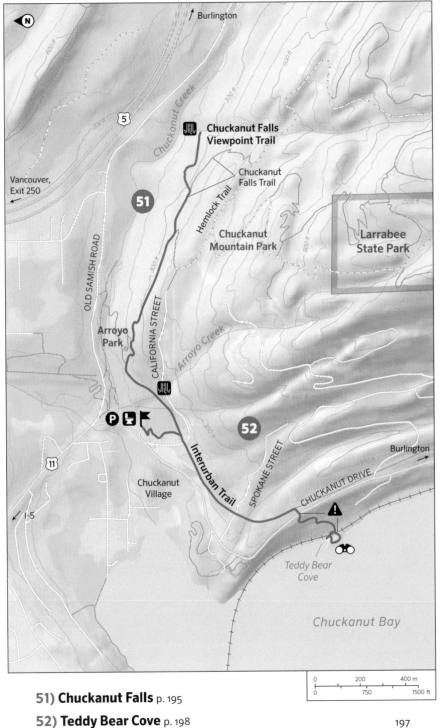

N

↑ Burlington

Chuckanut Creek

5

Chuckanut Falls
Viewpoint Trail

Chuckanut
Falls Trail

Vancouver,
Exit 250

51

Hemlock Trail

Chuckanut
Mountain Park

Larrabee
State Park

OLD SAMISH ROAD

CALIFORNIA STREET

Arroyo
Park

Arroyo Creek

P

52

11

Interurban Trail

SPOKANE STREET

Burlington →

CHUCKANUT DRIVE

I-5

Chuckanut
Village

Teddy Bear
Cove

Chuckanut Bay

0   200   400 m
0   750   1500 ft

52 Teddy Bear Cove | Trail map on p. 197

Distance: 2.6 km (1.6 mi)
Elevation gain: 65 m (210 ft)
High point: 70 m (230 ft)
Season: all year

Difficulty: ▪
Quality: ☺ ☺ ☺
Map: Square One Chuckanut
Recreation Area
Trailhead: 48°42'03" N, 122°29'21" W

FIRST OFF, it's called Teddy Bear Cove. Don't be surprised if the little ones insist on toting along a stuffed orca. You can pack the picnic and swimwear. Young beachcombers and train enthusiasts will particularly relish this coastal excursion.

GETTING THERE

Vehicle: On Interstate 5 in Bellingham, 41 km (25 mi) south of the Canada-U.S. border, take Exit 250. Head west on State Route 11 (Old Fairhaven Parkway). Sticking with SR 11, turn left on 12th Street and bear left onto Chuckanut Drive. Continue south for 2.1 km (1.3 mi). Turn left into the parking lot at the North Chuckanut Mountain trailhead (toilet available).

THE HIKE

From the trailhead in the City of Bellingham's Arroyo Park, head south on a gravel path, lined with sword ferns, and over a boardwalk. In 200 m (220 yd), turn right on the Interurban Trail and immediately cross California Street. The Interurban continues onto the wide gravel road ahead, paralleling Chuckanut Drive. It's private property, but an easement ensures public access (no parking). Watch out for local vehicle traffic as you pass homes and utility poles.

The Interurban Trail traces a portion of the historical electric rail line of the Bellingham and Skagit Interurban Railway, which provided passenger service between Bellingham and Mount Vernon from 1912 to 1928.

A pocket beach on Chuckanut Bay (dxʷšišəlčəb).

Cross Spokane Street by a fire hydrant and mailboxes. After 700 m (0.4 mi) on the Interurban Trail, a sign indicates the right-hand turn-off (48°41′40″ N, 122°29′38″ W) for Teddy Bear Cove. Descend steps to Chuckanut Drive, a Washington state scenic byway popular with drivers and cycle tourers, and carefully cross the busy road (no parking). Take stairs down to the big Teddy Bear Cove sign—a potential photo op involving plushies.

The Teddy Bear Cove Trail switchbacks down a wooded slope to a small headland, separated by a railroad, that juts into Chuckanut Bay (dxʷšišəlčəb in Lushootseed, the language of the Tulalip Tribes). When it's safe to do so, cross the BNSF Railway line, which is used by the Amtrak Cascades passenger trains that run between Vancouver, B.C., and Eugene, Oregon. On the other side of the track, head left or right to find stairs climbing the headland and stairs descending to pocket beaches on both ends.

No longer an unsanctioned nude beach, Teddy Bear Cove is a delightful place for a picnic, a swim, and some trainspotting. Waves lap against the sandstone cliffs, which are covered in ferns. Arbutus trees shed their cinnamon bark on top. The expansive view includes Chuckanut Island and Chuckanut Rock in Chuckanut Bay, Eliza Island and Lummi Island (Smemiekw in Xwlemi'chosen, the language of the Lummi Nation), and, beyond, the San Juan Islands in the Salish Sea.

Weathered sandstone on the beach at Teddy Bear Cove.

Hold young kids by the hand on the headland and beware of drop-offs. Watch out for broken glass on the sand-and-shell beaches, which may contain the remnants of middens from the historical bivalve harvests of Indigenous people. Retrace your steps for 1.3 km (0.8 mi) to the trailhead. Save some treats for the ascent back to Chuckanut Drive.

Dogs must be leashed on the Interurban Trail and at Teddy Bear Cove Park, which is administered by Whatcom County. No camping, fires, fireworks, or smoking.

·························· **Fun Fact** ··························

As well as connecting Bellingham's Fairhaven district and Larrabee State Park in Washington state, the Interurban Trail is part of the Coast Millennium Trail. The plan is to link White Rock, B.C., and Skagit County, Washington, with an 80-km (50-mi) trail across the Canada-U.S. border for hikers and cyclists.

53 | Rosario Head | Trail map on p. 204

Distance: 2.8 km (1.7 mi)
Elevation gain: 30 m (100 ft)
High point: 30 m (100 ft)
Season: all year

Difficulty: ●
Quality: ☺ ☺ ☺
Map: Green Trails 41S Deception Pass
Trailhead: 48°25′00″ N, 122°39′04″ W

WITH SPELLBINDING beaches, tide pools, and clifftop views, the Rosario Head Trail in Deception Pass State Park is heaven for parents and children. Sure, you can park right on its doorstep, but starting at Bowman Bay makes a wee hike of it—with huge rewards. Watch the water for California sea lions, harbour seals, and orcas.

GETTING THERE

Vehicle: On Interstate 5, 75 km (47 mi) south of the Canada-U.S. border, take Exit 230. Head west on State Route 20. In 18 km (11 mi), keep left at the SR 20 Spur junction in Anacortes, and continue 8.2 km (5.1 mi) on the SR 20 mainline. Alongside Pass Lake, turn right on Rosario Road (at the last intersection before SR 20 crosses the Deception Pass Bridge). Immediately, turn left on Bowman Bay Road. Finally, with the campground ahead, go left and pull into the gravel parking lot at the Bowman Bay boat launch (toilet available). Discover Pass required (purchase at pay station).

THE HIKE

Starting at the boat launch, head north on the grass behind the beach, past picnic tables and the Civilian Conservation Corps Interpretive Center (open April to September). Based in a one-time bathhouse, the centre spotlights the Depression-era public works crews that constructed roads, trails, and buildings in Deception Pass and many other state and national parks. Find the Bowman Bay/Rosario Beach Trail by a group picnic shelter and a huge, old-growth Douglas-fir.

Kʷəkʷáləlwət (The Maiden of Deception Pass) *on the tombolo.*

Take the wide path around the north end of the beach and up into the woods, keeping Bowman Bay in sight. Keep kids away from the trail's outer edge and ignore side paths. A metal fence guards the drop-off as you slice across a bluff front. Spot the guano-covered Gull Rocks and Coffin Rocks, at the mouth of Bowman Bay, and Deception Island beyond Northwest Pass.

Arrive at a grassy area and pass the Rosario Discovery Center, also housed in an old CCC bathhouse, where volunteer beach naturalists are based May to September. Bear left on a wide gravel path on the other side of the grass, going by picnic tables and joining the foot traffic from the nearby parking lot at the end of Rosario Beach Road.

Follow the Rosario Head Trail over the tombolo (sandy isthmus) leading to Rosario Head. A dock on the left provides moorage for boats in Sharpe Cove. Interpretive panels about sea stars and the intertidal zone flank an entrance to Rosario Beach on the right. Look for chitons, crabs, mussels, and sea anemones in the tide pools (no dogs allowed) at the south end of the idyllic arc of sand and pebbles. Stick to the intertidal rope trail installed to protect the tide pools from trampling.

Watching over the tombolo is Kʷəkʷáləlwət (The Maiden of Deception Pass), carved by Fidalgo Island artist Tracy Powell in collaboration with the Samish Nation and raised in 1983. The striking story pole and encircling panels (48°25′01″ N, 122°39′50″ W) share a legend, set at Rosario Beach, about the kinship between the Samish people and the ocean.

Urchin Rocks from Rosario Head.

Past Kʷəkʷálalwət (pronounced "Kwuh-kwal-uhl-wut"), take the path on the left into the trees to begin a clockwise loop on Rosario Head. A sign warns you to stay on the trail to avoid a potentially fatal fall; hold young kids by the hand. The main path curves gently up to the grassy bald atop the tied island, 1.4 km (0.9 mi) from your start. It's an incredible vantage point. Gaze over the entrance of Deception Pass to Whidbey Island, Northwest Pass to Deception Island, and Strait of Juan de Fuca to the Olympic Mountains. (Deception Pass is known as Xwchsónges in Xws7ámeshqen, the language of the Samish Nation, and sčudᶻ in Lushootseed, the language of the Tulalip Tribes.)

Continue on the path along the clifftop, keeping kids close. At the north end of the bald, descend steps and a rocky bit. Turn right, earn a view of Urchin Rocks, and bear left to pop out of the woods at Kʷəkʷálalwət. Retrace your steps to Bowman Bay.

Dogs must be leashed in Deception Pass State Park and are prohibited on swimming beaches. Drones require a permit.

···························· **Fun Fact** ·······················

A tombolo is a sand or gravel spit that ties an island to the mainland (or a larger island). Spits and tombolos are formed by longshore drift, which moves sand and other sediments parallel to the shore in the ocean's surf zone.

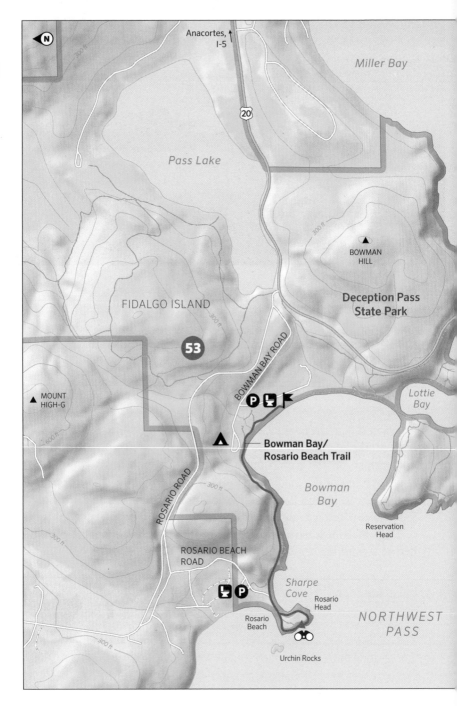

N

Anacortes,
I-5

Miller Bay

20

Pass Lake

▲ BOWMAN
HILL

**Deception Pass
State Park**

FIDALGO ISLAND

53

▲ MOUNT
HIGH-G

BOWMAN BAY ROAD

*Lottie
Bay*

P ♿ 🏕 ⚑

▲

— **Bowman Bay/
Rosario Beach Trail**

*Bowman
Bay*

ROSARIO ROAD

Reservation
Head

300 ft

ROSARIO BEACH
ROAD

*Sharpe
Cove*

♿ P

Rosario
Head

Rosario
Beach

*NORTHWEST
PASS*

👓

Urchin Rocks

53) Rosario Head p. 201 / **54) Goose Rock** p. 206

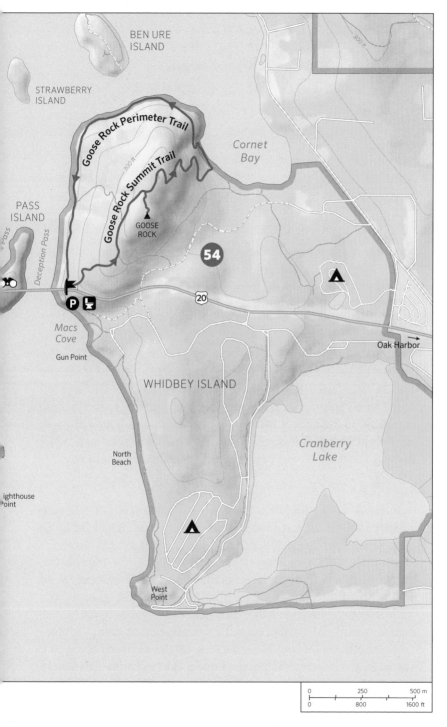

BEN URE
ISLAND

STRAWBERRY
ISLAND

Goose Rock Perimeter Trail

Cornet
Bay

Goose Rock Summit Trail

300 ft

PASS
ISLAND

GOOSE
ROCK

Deception Pass

Pass

54

Cornet
Bay

20

Macs
Cove

Gun Point

Oak Harbor

WHIDBEY ISLAND

North
Beach

Cranberry
Lake

ighthouse
oint

West
Point

| 0 | 250 | 500 m |
| 0 | 800 | 1600 ft |

54 Goose Rock | Trail map on p. 205

Distance: 3.6 km (2.2 mi)	**Difficulty:** ■
Elevation gain: 148 m (484 ft)	**Quality:** ☺ ☺ ☺
High point: 148 m (484 ft)	**Map:** Green Trails 41S Deception Pass
Season: all year	**Trailhead:** 48°24'18" N, 122°38'41" W

A DUO OF iconic bridges is reason enough to visit Deception Pass State Park. Add big trees, grassy balds, and blufftop views of the Salish Sea to the list with the fun hike to Goose Rock on Whidbey Island. You'll also get to tread a stretch of the Montana-to-Washington Pacific Northwest Trail.

GETTING THERE

Vehicle: On Interstate 5, 75 km (47 mi) south of the Canada-U.S. border, take Exit 230. Head west on State Route 20. In 18 km (11 mi), keep left at the SR 20 Spur junction in Anacortes, and continue 10 km (6.2 mi) on the SR 20 mainline to Whidbey Island. Immediately after crossing the Deception Pass Bridge, turn right into the "scenic vista" parking lot (toilet available). Discover Pass required (purchase at pay station).

THE HIKE

Before or after your hike, venture onto the lofty sidewalks of the Deception Pass Bridge and Canoe Pass Bridge for thrilling views of tidal currents, eddies, headlands, beaches, bald eagles, and kelp beds. Deception Pass and smaller Canoe Pass—separated by Pass Island—together constitute a gateway between the Strait of Juan de Fuca and Puget Sound, two of the three major bodies of the Salish Sea. Deception Pass is known as Xwchsónges in Xws7ámeshqen, the language of the Samish Nation, and sčudᶻ in Lushootseed, the language of the Tulalip Tribes.

To start the hike, head down the stairs at the north end of the parking lot. Go right at the bottom and under the Deception Pass Bridge,

A bald atop Goose Rock.

and quickly right again on the Goose Rock Summit Trail to commence a counterclockwise loop. Gain elevation on a wide path under sizable Douglas-firs and western red cedars. Pass a bench.

Choose left at a three-way junction. Take the next right fork. A sign asks visitors to preserve the sensitive meadows ahead by staying on established paths and stepping on bare rock. Head under the first power line, then follow the main trail right.

Hit a junction near the top of Goose Rock. Detour right for the glacier-abraded summit (48°24′05″ N, 122°38′23″ W) with its rocky, grassy bald, 900 m (0.6 mi) from the parking lot. Beware of drop-offs as you bask in blufftop views of the west coast of Whidbey Island, the Strait of Juan de Fuca, and the snow-capped Olympic Mountains. Bearberry, reindeer lichen, and arbutus grow in the shallow substrate.

Continue on the loop. Please respect the wooden barrier guarding the bald from damaging footsteps. Power lines sully the view from the next rise. The Goose Rock Summit Trail gets narrower and more rugged as it descends south, weaving back and forth on a steep slope. Keep kids close. Pass a precipitous partial viewpoint and hulking arbutus trees.

Meet the Goose Rock Perimeter Trail, a tiny leg of the long-distance Pacific Northwest Trail, at the hike's halfway point, with 1.8 km (1.1 mi) to go. (The PNT runs 1,900 km [1,200 mi] through Montana, Idaho, and Washington, from Glacier National Park to Cape Alava, the westernmost point in the conterminous U.S.) Turn left and parallel the shore of Cornet Bay opposite a marina, enjoying gorgeous scenery. Rise to cut across the front of a bluff. Unfortunately, the rumbling of U.S. military aircraft, such as the Boeing EA-18G Growler electronic-attack jet, based at Naval Air Station Whidbey Island, regularly pierces the tranquility.

Pass Ben Ure Island, and head into the woods. Overnight paddlers can reserve a state-park cabin on the island, which is named after a smuggler who dealt in Chinese immigrants in the late 1800s. Keep right at a signed junction. After going under the bridge, head up the stairs to the parking lot.

Dogs must be leashed in Deception Pass State Park, established in 1922 and now reputedly Washington's most-visited state park. No drones, fires, or mountain bikes. The Deception Pass Park Foundation raises money to support interpretive programs and restoration projects.

·················· **Fun Fact** ····················
The twig-and-leaf nest of a tree squirrel—such as the Douglas squirrel, found in Deception Pass State Park—is called a drey. Douglas squirrels are known to take over the empty nests of crows, hawks, and woodpeckers.

55 Young Hill

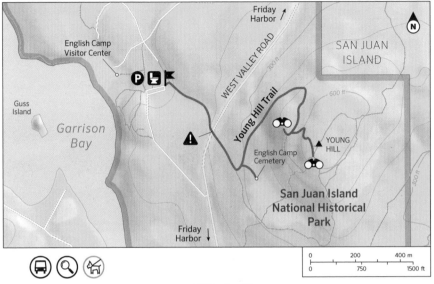

Distance: 3.2 km (2 mi)
Elevation gain: 170 m (560 ft)
High point: 198 m (650 ft)
Season: all year

Difficulty: ■
Quality: ☺ ☺
Map: USGS Roche Harbor
Trailhead: 48°35′11″ N, 123°08′49″ W

FROM A HILLTOP in Washington, peer across the Canada-U.S. maritime boundary at Vancouver Island and the Gulf Islands in B.C. On the way up, visit the graves of British soldiers on American soil. A hike to Young Hill on San Juan Island (Lháqemesh in Xws7ámeshqen, the language of the Samish Nation) highlights the Pacific Northwest's history of competing territorial claims. Be prepared for thought-provoking questions from curious young minds.

GETTING THERE

Transit: Take San Juan Transit from the Friday Harbor ferry loading lanes to English Camp.

The summit of Young Hill.

Vehicle: Washington State Ferries offers daily sailings between Anacortes and San Juan Island, and seasonal service to and from Sidney, B.C. From the Friday Harbor ferry dock, turn right on Front Street, left on Spring Street, and right on Second Street. Head northwest for 13 km (8.1 mi), continuing onto Guard Street, Beaverton Valley Road, and then West Valley Road. Enter San Juan Island National Historical Park. Turn left and follow the entrance road to the parking lot at English Camp (3905 West Valley Road; toilet available).

THE HIKE

In 1859, the U.S. and the United Kingdom came to the brink of war over the shooting of a Hudson's Bay Company hog on San Juan Island. After the Pig War crisis, the two empires carried out a joint military occupation of the island for a dozen years, with camps on opposite ends. Ultimately, the boundary dispute in the Salish Sea was arbitrated in favour of the U.S. without any human casualties. Our scenic outing explores English Camp, now preserved by San Juan Island National Historical Park, on the north end.

From the far side of the parking lot, head east on the Young Hill Trail in pleasant forest. Carefully cross West Valley Road and pass a service-road gate and kiosk. After 320 m (0.2 mi) on foot, detour right to visit the English Camp Cemetery. Surrounded by a white picket fence, gravestones commemorate several Royal Marines and one British civilian who died—the majority from drowning—in the 1860s during the occupation. The Royal Canadian Navy erected a plaque at the site on behalf of the Maritime Museum of B.C. in 1964.

Continue up the main trail, admiring twisted Garry oak and shedding arbutus trees on the grassy hillside. At the next fork, go right for an overlook. An interpretive panel identifies many features of the charmed landscape spread out before you, including Garrison Bay (Pe'pi'ow'elh in Xws7ámeshqen), the site of English Camp; Mosquito Pass; the Haro Strait, dividing Canada and the U.S.; and the Gulf Islands.

Return to the main trail, and boot it up the switchbacks to arrive on the summit of Young Hill (48°35′02″ N, 123°08′16″ W), the highest point in the park, 1.6 km (1 mi) from the trailhead. The view from the rocky, mossy bald is expansive. Scan the sky for bald eagles.

Head back the way you came. Stop by the English Camp visitor centre (open June to September), housed in the old Royal Marine barracks, to learn more about the area, occupied by Coast Salish people long before European contact.

Dogs must be leashed in San Juan Island National Historical Park, established in 1966. Camping, drones, and hunting are prohibited.

···················· **Fun Fact** ····················

The Canada-U.S. boundary extends 8,891 km (5,525 mi)— 5,061 km (3,145 mi) on land and 3,830 km (2,380 mi) on water. That's nearly the distance covered by an 11-hour flight between Vancouver and Shanghai. The International Boundary Commission maintains 5,528 boundary monuments and keeps clear a 6-m (20-ft) wide swath called the vista along the border.

||||||||||||||||||||||||||||| **Animals** |||||||||||||||||||||||||||||||||||||

FROM SEA TO SOIL TO SKY, the Pacific Northwest is home to an incredible array of creatures. A wildlife sighting can make a hike extra-memorable for kids. Challenge young ones to see how many of the featured animals—just a tiny sampling of what's out there—they can spot on the trails. Blow their minds with the faunal factoid included with each wildlife photograph.

The sixth principle of Leave No Trace is "Respect wildlife." Please do not approach, feed, harass, or touch wild animals, and keep kids close for safety. Never leave food scraps or garbage behind. Dogs should be leashed around wildlife, and keep them out of ponds, streams, and wetlands.

BLACK BEAR • *Ursus americanus*
Black bears (spá:th in Halq'eméylem, the language of the Stó:lō people) hibernate for three to five months every year, starting when the weather turns cold. On the B.C. coast, their dens are often in or under big trees, snags, logs, or stumps. Bears spend the summer and fall fattening up. When they go into the den in the fall, bears save energy by lowering their heart rate, breathing less oxygen, and dropping their body temperature. They survive by slowly burning through their fat reserves until they come out of the den in the spring.

BLUE DASHER •
Pachydiplax longipennis
Blue dashers are flesh-eating dragonflies. Adults eat damselflies, mosquitos, moths, and other dragonflies. As larvae, young blue dashers devour small fish, tadpoles, and invertebrates in and on the water.

BURROWING GREEN ANEMONE •
Anthopleura artemisia
Look for the burrowing green anemone in shallow sea water, buried in soft sediments. But keep your hands off its tentacles, which are covered in stinging cells that it uses to paralyze prey and fight off predators. This anemone gets its colour from a green alga.

CLARK'S NUTCRACKER •
Nucifraga columbiana
The Clark's nutcracker is a member of the crow family. It lives year-round on forested mountain slopes with plenty of ponderosa and whitebark pine trees (and cones). To get ready for winter, each bird stores tens of thousands of pine seeds in trees and in the ground.

BLACK-TAILED DEER ●

Odocoileus hemionus

When threatened, a black-tailed deer (húpit in sháshíshálem, the language of the shíshálh Nation) can warn other members of its species without making a sound. These deer release an alarm pheromone (a scent) from a gland on their back legs. Humans can't detect this "smell of fear."

NORTHERN ALLIGATOR LIZARD ●

Elgaria coerulea

Every year, northern alligator lizards go into brumation (hibernation for cold-blooded animals) for the cold season. When they wake in the spring, the lizards mate between mid-April and late May. They give birth to live young between mid-August and mid-September and then return to brumation.

OCHRE STAR ● *Pisaster ochraceus*

The ochre star is the most common intertidal sea star in B.C. and Washington. It can be purple, orange, or yellow, with white spines, and has five regenerating arms. An arm that is bitten off—by a sea otter, for example—can grow back in less than a year.

PACIFIC BANANA SLUG ●
Ariolimax columbianus
The Pacific banana slug is the second-largest land slug in the world—and the largest in North America. It grows up to 26 cm (10 in) long, or a little longer than your average banana! At its top speed of 16.5 cm (6.5 in) per minute, it covers a distance about the length of a Canadian banknote, making it also one of the slowest animals.

RAVEN ● *Corvus corax*
The raven (s̲kewk̲' in S̲kwx̲wú7mesh sníchim, the language of the Squamish Nation) is the largest songbird in the world. Considered one of the smartest birds, ravens speak to each other using dozens of different calls and can even recognize individual people. The raven is also superb at flying: It can do rolls and somersaults in the air as well as drop a stick and catch it before it hits the ground.

SOOTY GROUSE ●
Dendragapus fuliginosus
In the spring, listen for the deep hooting of the male sooty grouse (N̲I₃ED in SENĆOŦEN, the language of the W̲SÁNEĆ people) in the coastal forests of the Pacific Northwest. Males hoot to attract a female mate and mark their territory.

WESTERN TOAD • *Anaxyrus boreas*
Western toads live around shallow ponds, lakeshores, slow streams, marshes, bogs, and fens. They have a Bidder's organ, which sometimes allows (hermaphroditic) males to lay eggs. The western toad is a species of special concern in Canada.

YELLOW WARBLER •
Setophaga petechia
The yellow warbler feeds largely on caterpillars, which it finds in trees. This bird is known for its "sweet-sweet-sweet, sweeter-than-sweet" song.

IIIIIIIIIIIIIIIIIIIIIIIIIIIIIIII **Plants** IIIIIIIIIIIIIIIIIIIIIIIIIIIIIIIIII

FERNS, HORSETAILS, MOSSES, TREES—the variety of plants you might see on a hike is truly astonishing, especially if you pause to take a closer look as kids are wont to do. I've selected a dozen angiosperms (flowering plants) that I observed on the trails in this book. Impress the kids with the floral factoid accompanying each plant photograph.

Make sure kids don't eat random berries, which could be poisonous. Protect vegetation by staying on trails and not shortcutting. Flower picking and plant harvesting is illegal in B.C. provincial parks and Metro Vancouver regional parks.

ARCTIC LUPINE • *Lupinus arcticus*
Arctic lupine likes open areas, such as subalpine meadows and gravel bars, and can survive very cold winters. This wildflower's blue to purple petals are popular with butterflies.

BROAD-LEAVED STONECROP •
Sedum spathulifolium
Common on cliffs along the Salish Sea, broad-leaved stonecrop grows in mats. It has bright yellow petals and fleshy leaves. In the city, spot stonecrop in rock gardens.

COAST PENSTEMON ●

Penstemon serrulatus

Look for the blue to purple petals and saw-toothed leaves of coast penstemon on stream banks and rocky slopes above and below timberline. Penstemons are also known as beard-tongues. Can you see why? (Hint: Do you see an open mouth and a fuzzy tongue?)

FIREWEED ● *Epilobium angustifolium*
Fireweed (x̱ach't in Sḵwx̱wú7mesh sníchim, the language of the Squamish Nation) is Yukon's official flower, and it gets its name because it is common on land recovering from wildfires. Fireweed has magenta flowers that are popular with bees, which harvest the nectar and turn it into honey with a light flavour and colour.

Fireweed on Mount Thom (Hike 31).

GHOST PIPE ● *Monotropa uniflora*
Waxy-white from stem to flower, ghost pipe (*sq'awm peł tkéy'* in Nłeʔkepmxcín, the language of the Nlaka'pamux people) is easy to mistake for a fungus. It's a myco-heterotroph—a plant that gets its food from fungi around tree roots rather than making its own food with sunlight, carbon dioxide, and water.

HEART-LEAVED ARNICA ●
Arnica cordifolia
Common in B.C. east of the Coast and Cascade Mountains, heart-leaved arnica (*ntsetsahsmnw'íxʷ* in Nsyilxcən, the language of the Syilx people) shows off its bright yellow flowers in meadows and forests at mid- to high elevations. Many *Arnica* species, including this one, are sources of medicine.

HOOKER'S FAIRYBELLS ●
Prosartes hookeri
Also known as drops-of-gold, Hooker's fairybells have creamy-white, slender, bell-like flowers. They grow in moist, shady forests from sea level to mountain slopes. Notice the leaves of these plants, which are designed to protect the flowers: They channel water away and keep slugs and snails at bay.

KING GENTIAN ● *Gentiana sceptrum*
The large blue petals of king gentian are found in bogs, moist meadows, and lakeshores at low to mid-elevations from B.C. to northern California. Blue Gentian Lake (Lost Lake, Hike 7) has lots of them. *Gentian* is pronounced "jen-shuhn."

PINK MONKEY-FLOWER ●
Mimulus lewisii
Pink monkey-flower has lovely pink-purple to rose-red petals. Spot these bright flowers along wet stream banks, meadows, and avalanche tracks from California to Alaska.

TIGER LILY ● *Lilium columbianum*
Tiger lily (cágʷičəd in Lushootseed, the language of the Tulalip Tribes) flowers are yellow-orange to reddish-orange with dark red or purple spots. This wildflower is common in open forests, meadows, and clearings and on the sides of many roads.

SALMONBERRY • *Rubus spectabilis*
Salmonberry (elílá:lhp in Halq'eméylem, the language of the Stó:lō people) has rosy red to reddish-purple flowers and its yellow, orange, or red fruit look like raspberries. The berries ripen early, often in May. To the Stó:lō, the salmonberry shrubs are a natural calendar: Salmon runs in the Fraser River are calculated based on when the shrubs blossom, fruit, and shed their leaves. Salmonberry is common along the coast in B.C. and west of the Cascade Range in Washington and Oregon.

WESTERN PASQUEFLOWER •
Pulsatilla occidentalis
Western pasqueflower blooms in early spring, soon after the snow melts. When the white or purple flowers fade, it grows a mop-top seed head that looks like it belongs in a children's book by Dr. Seuss. It's a member of the buttercup family.

|||||||||||||||||||||||||||||||||| **Fungi** ||||||||||||||||||||||||||||||||||

WHILE WALKING in the forest it's fun to spot the short-lived sporocarp (fruiting body) of fungi that grows above ground on dirt, trees, and rotting logs. Many species have a cap and stem like the toadstools in picture books. What we don't see is the mycelium (vegetative body), which lies hidden either inside the tree or in wood under the ground. I've included a fungal factoid with each mushroom photograph.

Beware of poisonous mushrooms, which may look a lot like edible varieties. Mushroom picking is illegal in B.C. provincial parks and Metro Vancouver regional parks. Leave them to do their essential jobs as the leading decomposers and recyclers of the natural world.

||||||||||||||||||||||||||||||||||||||||||||||||||||||||||||||||||||||||||||||||

ADMIRABLE BOLETE ●
Aureoboletus mirabilis
The admirable bolete grows on and around rotting hemlock logs and stumps. It has a large maroon brown cap and stem and yellow pores. This bolete's lemony flavour makes it a favourite of mycophiles (mushroom enthusiasts).

ANGEL-WINGS ●
Pleurocybella porrigens
The smooth white caps of angel-wings are often found in clusters. They're easy to spot on decaying softwood, particularly hemlock logs and stumps.

CHICKEN OF THE WOODS ●
Laetiporus sulphureus
Chicken of the woods has a bright orange cap that grows like shelves on older conifers or deadwood. It is said to taste like chicken.

FUNNEL-CAP ● *Clitocybe gibba*
The funnel-cap breaks down fallen leaves on the forest floor. When it is mature, the pale pinkish tan cap lives up to the mushroom's name.

EYELASH PIXIE CUP ●
Scutellinia scutellata
The eyelash pixie cup has a small, bright-red fruiting body. It gets its name from the long, dark brown hairs or "eyelashes" on its outer surface. Look for clusters of pixie cups on rotting wood or soil.

INKY-CAP ● *Coprinopsis atramentaria*
When it's mature, the lead-grey to brownish cap of the inky-cap absorbs moisture from the air and turns to black goo. This process is called deliquescence. They often grow in clusters.

KING BOLETE ● *Boletus edulis*
The thick stem of the king bolete supports a hefty yellowish to reddish brown cap. It grows on the ground under trees and is found around the world. Chefs know this mushroom by names such as cèpe, porcini, and penny bun.

LILAC CONIFER ●
Cortinarius traganus
The lilac conifer has a fruity smell. However, its pale lilac to blue-lilac cap and stem are what'll get your attention.

SUMMER OYSTER MUSHROOM ●
Pleurotus pulmonarius
The summer oyster is the most common oyster mushroom in the Pacific Northwest. It grows like shingles on all kinds of trees, dead or alive. And it is one of the few carnivorous mushrooms: It eats bacteria and small roundworms called nematodes.

VIOLET CORT ● *Cortinarius violaceus*
Also known as the violet webcap, the violet cort has a dark purple to nearly black cap. It smells mildly of cedar.

WOOD WOOLLY-FOOT ●
Gymnopus peronatus
The wood woolly-foot grows a brownish to ochre-coloured cap. It likes dead leaves and needles on the forest floor and is widespread at lower elevations.

Acknowledgements

||||||||||||||||||||||||||||||||||||||||||||||||||||||||||||||||||||||||||||||||||||||||||||

AS WITH MOST things in life, trail research is better with good company. Special thanks to Jaime Adams, Jacqueline Ashby, Esther Brysch, Julius Brysch, Stefan Brysch, Verena Brysch, Patrick Hui, Joan Septembre, and Svetlana Tkacova. Many thanks also to Dawn Coers, Richard Egolf, Susana Egolf, Tara Henley, Laszlo Hulicsko, Amanda Lewis, Leanna McLennan, Louise Morrin, Sarah Palmer, Erin Pedersen, Stephanie Septembre, and Stephen Thomson.

It's always a pleasure to work with Rob Sanders, Jennifer Croll, Megan Jones, Makenzie Pratt, Lara LeMoal, and the rest of the talented team at Greystone Books. I'm grateful to Lucy Kenward—the best editor a hiking guidebook author could ask for. Full credit goes to Jessica Sullivan for the beautiful book design. Thanks to Richard Vladars for a fine cartographic collaboration, and to copy editor Erin Parker and proofreader Alison Strobel for catching my errors.

For me, one of the rewards of writing a hiking guidebook is the opportunity to learn about the culture, ecology, geography, geology, and history of the trails. Place names in Indigenous languages are drawn from interactive maps produced by Kwi Awt Stelmexw, the Musqueam Nation, Samish Nation, and Tulalip Tribes; the work of the Squamish Líỉwat Cultural Centre and Stó:lō Research and Resource Management Centre; and other definitive sources. I'm indebted to Myia Antone, for helping start the book off on the right foot, as well as Cecilia Point, who wrote a generous foreword for *Destination Hikes In and Around Southwestern British Columbia*.

Ollie's first hike, in the Lower Seymour Conservation Reserve.

Several outdoor programs had a significant impact on me during my formative years. It seems fitting to acknowledge them in these pages: the YMCA of Greater Vancouver's Camp Howdy, the Evans Lake Forest Education Centre (via Harbour View Elementary School), the 5th Burnaby Mountain Scout Troop (Don Francis), the Harrison Hike (Charles Hou) and Outdoors Club (Jim Stockman and Eric Walton) at Burnaby North Secondary School, and an environmental film project supported by the Evergreen Foundation (Charlotte Gaudette). I owe some of my fondest hiking memories to high-school classmates and early trail partners John Drewoth, Anna Janecka, and Peggy Yen.

The Wanderung Outdoor Recreation Society's directors, trip organizers, and participants have my sincere appreciation for nurturing a wonderful community of carpooling outdoor recreationists who hit the trail in small groups. Thanks also to David Scanlon of the British Columbia Mountaineering Club. I'm grateful to Nicole Reid, Lydia Kwa, Jamie Sullivan, Charles Demers, and Cara Ng, as well as Kelly O'Connor, Karen Tam Wu, Josha MacNab, and all of my former coworkers at the Pembina Institute, for support and encouragement along the way.

Last but certainly not least, a big thank-you to my son, Ollie, for joining me on this journey. This book is for you.

Best Hikes by Category

WONDERING WHERE TO GO? To help you quickly choose a destination, I've nominated up to five hikes in each of 10 categories. My picks are not ranked; they're listed in order of hike number.

#	Hike	Region	Season
BEST HIKES FOR BIG TREES			
5	Capilano Canyon	North Vancouver	all year
6	Cypress Falls	West Vancouver and Lions Bay	all year
9	Erin Moore Trail	West Vancouver and Lions Bay	all year
19	Ancient Cedars Trail	Whistler	late spring to early fall
44	Skookumchuck Narrows	Sunshine Coast	all year
BEST HIKES FOR CAR CAMPING			
10	Four Lakes Trail	Squamish	all year
26	Lower Falls Trail	Maple Ridge	most of the year
30	Hicks Lake	Mission to Harrison Hot Springs	all year
37	Flash Lake	E.C. Manning Provincial Park	late spring to early fall
45	Gray Peninsula	Gulf Islands	all year
BEST HIKES FOR FIRST-TIMERS			
3	Rice Lake	North Vancouver	all year
10	Four Lakes Trail	Squamish	all year
23	Sasamat Lake	Burnaby to Coquitlam	all year
26	Lower Falls Trail	Maple Ridge	most of the year
32	Three Bears	Chilliwack	all year
BEST HIKES FOR GEOLOGY			
14	Berg Lake	Squamish	summer
41	Homesite Caves	Sunshine Coast	all year
46	Pebble Beach	Gulf Islands	all year
49	Sooke Potholes	Victoria	all year

#	Hike	Region	Season
BEST HIKES FOR HISTORY			
2	Fisherman's Trail	North Vancouver	all year
16	Train Wreck Falls	Whistler	spring to fall
18	Parkhurst Ghost Town	Whistler	spring to fall
27	Railway Trail	Mission to Harrison Hot Springs	all year
55	Young Hill	Anacortes and San Juan Islands	all year
BEST HIKES FOR PEAK BAGGERS			
31	Mount Thom	Chilliwack	all year
42	Pender Hill	Sunshine Coast	all year
54	Goose Rock	Anacortes and San Juan Islands	all year
55	Young Hill	Anacortes and San Juan Islands	all year
BEST HIKES FOR SUSPENSION BRIDGES			
2	Fisherman's Trail	North Vancouver	all year
4	Lynn Canyon	North Vancouver	all year
15	Cal-Cheak Trail	Whistler	spring to fall
16	Train Wreck Falls	Whistler	spring to fall
BEST HIKES FOR TIDE POOLS			
22	Jug Island Beach	Burnaby to Coquitlam	all year
45	Gray Peninsula	Gulf Islands	all year
46	Pebble Beach	Gulf Islands	all year
48	McKenzie Bight	Victoria	all year
53	Rosario Head	Anacortes and San Juan Islands	all year
BEST HIKES FOR TRANSIT			
4	Lynn Canyon	North Vancouver	all year
6	Cypress Falls	West Vancouver and Lions Bay	all year
21	Burnaby Mountain	Burnaby to Coquitlam	all year
38	Dorman Point	Howe Sound	all year
39	Killarney Lake	Howe Sound	all year
BEST HIKES FOR WATERFALLS			
16	Train Wreck Falls	Whistler	spring to fall
26	Lower Falls Trail	Maple Ridge	most of the year
28	Steelhead Falls	Mission to Harrison Hot Springs	all year
40	Chapman Falls	Sunshine Coast	all year
49	Sooke Potholes	Victoria	all year

#	Hike	Distance
41	Homesite Caves	1.4 km (0.9 mi)
42	Pender Hill	1.6 km (1 mi)
45	Gray Peninsula	2.2 km (1.4 mi)
32	Three Bears	2.3 km (1.4 mi)
38	Dorman Point	2.4 km (1.5 mi)
52	Teddy Bear Cove	2.6 km (1.6 mi)
16	Train Wreck Falls	2.8 km (1.7 mi)
53	Rosario Head	2.8 km (1.7 mi)
3	Rice Lake	3 km (1.9 mi)
4	Lynn Canyon	3 km (1.9 mi)
6	Cypress Falls	3 km (1.9 mi)
48	McKenzie Bight	3 km (1.9 mi)
9	Erin Moore Trail	3.2 km (2 mi)
15	Cal-Cheak Trail	3.2 km (2 mi)
17	One Duck Lake	3.2 km (2 mi)
23	Sasamat Lake	3.2 km (2 mi)
35	Little Douglas Lake	3.2 km (2 mi)
55	Young Hill	3.2 km (2 mi)
11	Brohm Lake	3.5 km (2.2 mi)
54	Goose Rock	3.6 km (2.2 mi)
51	Chuckanut Falls	3.8 km (2.4 mi)
14	Berg Lake	3.9 km (2.4 mi)
5	Capilano Canyon	4.1 km (2.5 mi)
47	Echo Valley Trail	4.2 km (2.6 mi)
49	Sooke Potholes	4.2 km (2.6 mi)
8	Bowen Lookout	4.3 km (2.7 mi)
20	Holly Lake	4.3 km (2.7 mi)
19	Ancient Cedars Trail	4.7 km (2.9 mi)

#	Hike	Distance
1	Dog Mountain	4.8 km (3 mi)
34	Thacker Mountain	4.8 km (3 mi)
36	Similkameen Trail	4.8 km (3 mi)
28	Steelhead Falls	5 km (3.1 mi)
22	Jug Island Beach	5.2 km (3.2 mi)
50	Lummi Peak	5.3 km (3.3 mi)
33	Thaletel Trail	5.4 km (3.4 mi)
18	Parkhurst Ghost Town	5.6 km (3.5 mi)
26	Lower Falls Trail	5.7 km (3.5 mi)
10	Four Lakes Trail	6 km (3.7 mi)
30	Hicks Lake	6 km (3.7 mi)
21	Burnaby Mountain	6.5 km (4 mi)
43	Klein Lake	6.5 km (4 mi)
46	Pebble Beach	6.5 km (4 mi)
13	Cheakamus Canyon	7 km (4.3 mi)
31	Mount Thom	7 km (4.3 mi)
12	Levette Lake	8 km (5 mi)
29	Hoover Lake	8 km (5 mi)
39	Killarney Lake	8 km (5 mi)
44	Skookumchuck Narrows	8 km (5 mi)
7	Lost Lake	8.5 km (5.3 mi)
24	Woodland Walk	9 km (5.6 mi)
40	Chapman Falls	9 km (5.6 mi)
37	Flash Lake	10 km (6.2 mi)
25	Alouette Valley Trail	12 km (7.5 mi)
27	Railway Trail	12 km (7.5 mi)
2	Fisherman's Trail	16 km (10 mi)

Hikes by Elevation Gain

#	Hike	Elevation Gain
23	Sasamat Lake	20 m (65 ft)
3	Rice Lake	30 m (100 ft)
36	Similkameen Trail	30 m (100 ft)
53	Rosario Head	30 m (100 ft)
11	Brohm Lake	40 m (130 ft)
41	Homesite Caves	40 m (130 ft)
45	Gray Peninsula	40 m (130 ft)
1	Dog Mountain	45 m (150 ft)
15	Cal-Cheak Trail	45 m (150 ft)
30	Hicks Lake	45 m (150 ft)
37	Flash Lake	45 m (150 ft)
16	Train Wreck Falls	50 m (165 ft)
32	Three Bears	50 m (165 ft)
5	Capilano Canyon	60 m (200 ft)
39	Killarney Lake	60 m (200 ft)
44	Skookumchuck Narrows	60 m (200 ft)
49	Sooke Potholes	60 m (200 ft)
27	Railway Trail	65 m (210 ft)
47	Echo Valley Trail	65 m (210 ft)
52	Teddy Bear Cove	65 m (210 ft)
46	Pebble Beach	75 m (250 ft)
18	Parkhurst Ghost Town	80 m (260 ft)
28	Steelhead Falls	80 m (260 ft)
22	Jug Island Beach	85 m (280 ft)
2	Fisherman's Trail	90 m (295 ft)
17	One Duck Lake	90 m (295 ft)
35	Little Douglas Lake	90 m (295 ft)
38	Dorman Point	100 m (330 ft)

#	Hike	Elevation Gain
51	Chuckanut Falls	100 m (330 ft)
25	Alouette Valley Trail	110 m (360 ft)
26	Lower Falls Trail	115 m (380 ft)
6	Cypress Falls	120 m (390 ft)
8	Bowen Lookout	120 m (390 ft)
10	Four Lakes Trail	120 m (390 ft)
40	Chapman Falls	120 m (390 ft)
34	Thacker Mountain	130 m (430 ft)
14	Berg Lake	140 m (460 ft)
54	Goose Rock	148 m (484 ft)
43	Klein Lake	150 m (490 ft)
48	McKenzie Bight	150 m (490 ft)
9	Erin Moore Trail	155 m (510 ft)
4	Lynn Canyon	170 m (560 ft)
42	Pender Hill	170 m (560 ft)
55	Young Hill	170 m (560 ft)
24	Woodland Walk	175 m (575 ft)
7	Lost Lake	180 m (590 ft)
19	Ancient Cedars Trail	189 m (620 ft)
13	Cheakamus Canyon	235 m (770 ft)
20	Holly Lake	245 m (800 ft)
33	Thaletel Trail	250 m (820 ft)
21	Burnaby Mountain	290 m (950 ft)
31	Mount Thom	290 m (950 ft)
29	Hoover Lake	300 m (985 ft)
12	Levette Lake	300 m (985 ft)
50	Lummi Peak	310 m (1,020 ft)

A boardwalk on the Sasamat Lake Loop Trail (Hike 23), with Mount Seymour in the background.

Bibliography

Bates, Dawn, Thom Hess, and Vi Hilbert. *Lushootseed Dictionary*. Seattle: University of Washington Press, 1994.

Beaumont, Ronald C. *Sechelt Dictionary*. Sechelt: Sechelt Indian Band, 2011.

Galloway, Brent D. *Dictionary of Upriver Halkomelem*. 2 vols. University of California Publications in Linguistics. Berkeley: University of California Press, 2009.

Hui, Stephen. *Destination Hikes In and Around Southwestern British Columbia: Swimming Holes, Mountain Peaks, Waterfalls, and More*. Vancouver: Greystone Books, 2021.

Hui, Stephen. *105 Hikes In and Around Southwestern British Columbia*. Vancouver: Greystone Books, 2018.

Lillooet Hiking Guide: Canyon to Alpine. 2nd ed. Lillooet: Lillooet Naturalist Society, 2011.

Litzenberger, Lyle. *Burke and Widgeon: A Hiker's Guide*. Port Coquitlam: Pebblestone Publishing, 2013.

Mansbridge, Francis. *Hollyburn: The Mountain & the City*. Vancouver: Ronsdale Press, 2008.

Oprsal, Peter, and Ryan Robertson. *Whistler Mountain Bike Trail Guide*. Whistler: bikepirate, 2015.

Sept, J. Duane. *Common Mushrooms of the Northwest*. Rev. ed. Sechelt: Calypso Publishing, 2012.

Squamish Nation Dictionary Project. Sḵwx̱wú7mesh Sníchim—Xwelíten Sníchim Sḵexwts: Squamish—English Dictionary. North Vancouver: Squamish Nation Education Department; Seattle: University of Washington Press, 2011.

Stoltmann, Randy. *Hiking Guide to the Big Trees of Southwestern British Columbia.* Vancouver: Western Canada Wilderness Committee, 1987.

Tracey, David. *Vancouver Tree Book: A Living City Field Guide.* Vancouver: Pure Wave Media, 2016.

Turner, Nancy J. *Ancient Pathways, Ancestral Knowledge: Ethnobotany and Ecological Wisdom of Indigenous Peoples of Northwestern North America.* 2 vols. McGill-Queen's Indigenous and Northern Studies. Montréal: McGill-Queen's University Press, 2014.

Varner, Collin. *The Flora and Fauna of Coastal British Columbia and the Pacific Northwest.* Victoria: Heritage House Publishing, 2018.

Wheater, Rich. *Vancouver Rock Climbing.* Squamish: Quickdraw Publications, 2015.

Where Rivers, Mountains and People Meet: Squamish Líĺwat Cultural Centre. Whistler: Spo7ez Cultural Centre and Community Society, 2010.

Index

Train Wreck Bridge (Hike 16) spans the Cheakamus River (Ch'iyákmesh Staḵw).

Atop the Twin Sisters (Ch'ich'iyúy). PHOTO: ALEXANDRA JUZKIW

About the Author and Photographer

STEPHEN HUI has been hiking, backpacking, and scrambling in British Columbia's Coast Mountains for 30 years. He's the author of 105 *Hikes In and Around Southwestern British Columbia* and *Destination Hikes In and Around Southwestern British Columbia*, both #1 B.C. bestsellers. His outdoor writing and photography have appeared in the *Georgia Straight*, *Toronto Sun*, *Le Journal de Montréal*, and *Burnaby Now*.

Hui lives in Vancouver, B.C.—in the territories of the Musqueam, Squamish, and Tsleil-Waututh First Nations—with his son, Ollie. *Best Hikes and Nature Walks With Kids In and Around Southwestern British Columbia* is his third book. Hui is currently undertaking field research for the forthcoming second edition of 105 *Hikes*.

A portion of the author's royalties from this book will go to Take a Hike Foundation, supporting vulnerable youth in B.C. with a full-time mental health and emotional well-being program embedded in public schools.

105hikes.com

 @BestHikesBC

 @stephenhui

 @StephenHui

 @105hikes

 stephen@105hikes.com

 #BestHikesWithKidsBC